Java: The Good Parts

Java: The Good Parts

Jim Waldo

O'REILLY®

Beijing · Cambridge · Farnham · Köln · Sebastopol · Taipei · Tokyo

Java: The Good Parts
by Jim Waldo

Copyright © 2010 Jim Waldo. All rights reserved.
Printed in the United States of America.

Published by O'Reilly Media, Inc., 1005 Gravenstein Highway North, Sebastopol, CA 95472.

O'Reilly books may be purchased for educational, business, or sales promotional use. Online editions are also available for most titles (*http://my.safaribooksonline.com*). For more information, contact our corporate/institutional sales department: 800-998-9938 or *corporate@oreilly.com*.

Editor: Mike Loukides
Production Editor: Kristen Borg
Copyeditor: Genevieve d'Entremont
Proofreader: Kristen Borg

Indexer: Fred Brown
Cover Designer: Karen Montgomery
Interior Designer: David Futato
Illustrator: Robert Romano

Printing History:

May 2010:	First Edition.

 This book uses RepKover™, a durable and flexible lay-flat binding.

ISBN: 978-0-596-80373-5

[M]

1271431316

Table of Contents

Preface

This is yet another book about the Java Programming Language and the Java Programming Environment. As one of the most popular programming languages in use today, Java has already been the subject of a lot of books. On the day this sentence was written, a search on Amazon for books about "Java programming" returned 11,978 results. So why does there need to be another?

The premise of this book is that Java, after some 15 years of development, has become a large and rather complex language and environment. The language itself has seen considerable growth since the time it was introduced. The libraries associated with the language have grown even more, and the requirements of upward compatibility have meant that while many things have been added, very little has been taken away. The curse of any major piece of software is that to survive, it must become popular, but in becoming popular, the software is required not to change in such a way that it would break things that depend upon it. This would be fine if software could be made perfect from the start, but it doesn't work that way. All software is an attempt to get things right, and each attempt is more or less successful. Even if a piece of software were perfect when it was first released, users would find new ways to use that software (or the environment in which it was used would change) so that it would not remain perfect. So we (the programmers) try to make the software better, which means that we add things, which means that over time, all software is subject to a buildup of crud.

This book is an attempt to pick out some of the very best parts about Java (both the language and the environment) and talk about how to use those parts and why they are good. This isn't to say that the parts of Java that won't be talked about in this book aren't good; it means that the parts I will be talking about differentiate Java from many other languages, and do so in a way that makes Java particularly valuable for the kind of work I and many software engineers do.

Java and Me

My own history with Java goes back to when I first joined Sun Labs* in March of 1992. At that time, there was a secret project, part of which was a new programming language. The language, then called Oak, was a variant of C++ designed for work in embedded devices, but it seemed to have some promise as a general-purpose language. At that time, there were a lot of projects that were looking at alternative object-oriented system languages. The dominant language of that ilk was C++, but there was considerable dissatisfaction with the complexity that was beginning to accrue to that language (and this was before the addition of templates).

I looked at the Oak language, but at the time, it seemed too unstable to be a reasonable tool for the work I was starting to do in distributed systems. Adopting it for our work would have been an example of what was known in the lab as *Error 33*, the error of basing the success of one research project on the success of a different, as yet unfinished, research project. I filed away the documentation on the language, and my group moved on, doing our research in Modula-3.

I next saw Java about 18 months later, as part of an internal review exercise known as Language Day. By then, the Oak language was the only surviving part of the earlier, larger project on embedded systems, and had moved to Sun Labs as its organizational home. Burt Sutherland, the director of Sun Labs, realized that he had at least four language projects going on in his small lab, and so organized a day in which each of the projects could be presented. His hope was to give each project some exposure, and perhaps to get some cross-fertilization and consolidation among the projects. As the lead of a group that was using yet another language, I was invited to participate as well.

I'm not sure what the official result of Language Day was, but it did give me a second look at Oak, which had matured and stabilized considerably since I had last seen it. My group was looking for a new language at the time, since support for Modula-3 was becoming harder and harder to get. So we decided to switch our research language to Oak. At the time, it seemed like a minor (and only somewhat risky) instance of Error 33; I remember writing an email to the lab director arguing that it was acceptable for my group to be using Oak, because as a research group, it was all right for us to use a language that wasn't commercially viable.

This was just a couple of months before Oak became Java, before applets were first seen in a browser, and before Java as a language and an environment exploded. I became part of a Sun-wide group (headed by Bill Joy) that tried to plot out the trajectory of the language. I was also asked to be part of a group doing the first formal review of the language, which led to some changes to the basic language design.

---

* Officially, Sun Microsystems Laboratories, Inc.

It is hard to remember those early days when Java went from an obscure programming language to a phenomenon seemingly overnight. For those who knew anything about the language, or even just wanted in on the excitement, it became an all-hands-on-deck experience. This was also the time that the World Wide Web was growing exponentially, and the growth of the Web and the growth of Java seemed to be somehow joined. Developments in the language became national news. I can't remember anything like it before or since.

My group was soon pulled out of Sun Labs to become the core of the East Coast branch of the Java software organization, working on some of the distributed libraries for Java. While I've floated around various parts of Sun over the last 15 years (and am now back where I started, in Sun Labs), I've not switched my main language in that time. I've participated in internal discussions of what was to be added to the language and the libraries, saw the formation of the Java Community Process, and saw the platform split into Enterprise, Standard, and Micro editions. I've given more talks at JavaOne than there have been JavaOnes, and have also given talks on Java at conferences in Japan, Italy, and England.

During all of this, I've spent a lot of time thinking about what makes Java an interesting or enjoyable language and environment in which to work, and what parts of the language get in the way of that interest and enjoyment. I've argued, both successfully and not, for the inclusion or exclusion of certain features. And I've written a fair amount of code, and read far more, often written by engineers who are far more expressive with the language than I. Java is not the only language that I use, but when I turn to some other and then return, it is like coming home—I always feel comfortable, even if there are quirks and topics that need to be avoided.

You, the Audience

This book is not intended as a mechanism for teaching the reader Java. I assume that you are familiar with the syntax of the language and the basic concepts of object-oriented programming. I also assume that you have some background in the libraries that make up the Java language. The intent of this book is not to teach you completely new things, but to remind you of things that you already knew but may have forgotten, or to get you to see things that you had already thought about in a new light. For those who are just starting with Java, I hope that this book can show some features that you should learn first. For the experienced Java programmer, I hope that this book will serve as a focusing function. You may have different parts of the language that you think are the good parts, or you may think that some things I like are features that make the language worse. But if this book can get you to think about what is good and not so good in the language, then it serves its purpose.

Conventions Used in This Book

The following typographical conventions are used in this book:

Italic
> Indicates new terms, URLs, email addresses, filenames, and file extensions.

`Constant width`
> Used for program listings, as well as within paragraphs to refer to program elements such as variable or function names, databases, data types, environment variables, statements, and keywords.

`Constant width bold`
> Shows commands or other text that should be typed literally by the user.

`Constant width italic`
> Shows text that should be replaced with user-supplied values or by values determined by context.

Using Code Examples

This book is here to help you get your job done. In general, you may use the code in this book in your programs and documentation. You do not need to contact us for permission unless you're reproducing a significant portion of the code. For example, writing a program that uses several chunks of code from this book does not require permission. Selling or distributing a CD-ROM of examples from O'Reilly books does require permission. Answering a question by citing this book and quoting example code does not require permission. Incorporating a significant amount of example code from this book into your product's documentation does require permission.

We appreciate, but do not require, attribution. An attribution usually includes the title, author, publisher, and ISBN. For example: "*Java: The Good Parts*, by Jim Waldo. Copyright 2010 Jim Waldo, 978-0-596-80373-5."

If you feel your use of code examples falls outside fair use or the permission given here, feel free to contact us at *permissions@oreilly.com*.

How to Contact Us

Please address comments and questions concerning this book to the publisher:

> O'Reilly Media, Inc.
> 1005 Gravenstein Highway North
> Sebastopol, CA 95472
> 800-998-9938 (in the United States or Canada)
> 707-829-0515 (international or local)
> 707-829-0104 (fax)

We have a web page for this book, where we list errata, examples, and any additional information. You can access this page at:

http://oreilly.com/catalog/9780596803735

To comment or ask technical questions about this book, send email to:

bookquestions@oreilly.com

For more information about our books, conferences, Resource Centers, and the O'Reilly Network, see our website at:

http://oreilly.com

Safari® Books Online

Safari Safari Books Online is an on-demand digital library that lets you easily
Books Online search over 7,500 technology and creative reference books and videos to find the answers you need quickly.

With a subscription, you can read any page and watch any video from our library online. Read books on your cell phone and mobile devices. Access new titles before they are available for print, and get exclusive access to manuscripts in development and post feedback for the authors. Copy and paste code samples, organize your favorites, download chapters, bookmark key sections, create notes, print out pages, and benefit from tons of other time-saving features.

O'Reilly Media has uploaded this book to the Safari Books Online service. To have full digital access to this book and others on similar topics from O'Reilly and other publishers, sign up for free at *http://my.safaribooksonline.com*.

Acknowledgments

One of the best things about participating in the last 15 years of Java development has been the cast of characters that it brought me into contact with. James Gosling built a beautiful language and attracted quite a varied group of engineers, managers, marketing people, and assorted others. There were many who were brilliant, some less so, but they were all interesting. There were heroes and villains, sinners and saints, and all sorts in between. Some became good friends, others became worthy adversaries, but all contributed to the language, the environment, and the experience.

Any acknowledgment that singles out one or more of them by name would be unfair, idiosyncratic, and incomplete, even if it is just those who I remember being particularly important to me. But I'll do it anyway. The ones that I remember best and most fondly are those who I worked with most closely, and include John McClain, Peter Jones, and Ann Wollrath. Without them, my understanding of Java would be very different than it is now.

I must also acknowledge the support and forbearance of my wife, Susan Mitchell, whose encouragement and support (and willingness to allow me to disappear for long periods of time when I was supposedly not at work) made this book, and so much more, possible.

Any project of this size requires a cheerleader, scold, and sounding board; Mike Loukides, my editor at O'Reilly, filled all of these roles and others. I would also like to thank my technical reviewers who found numerous places that would have been embarrassing had they been committed to print. The book is better because of them; where it is not, the fault is mine.

Finally, I would like to dedicate this book to the memory of Sun Microsystems, Inc., the company that was the home of the original Java development. It was never clear in the progress of Java (and much else) what was intended and what happened in spite of the best efforts of the organization. But the results were sometimes spectacular, and it was one hell of a ride. I miss it already.

CHAPTER 1

An Introduction to Java

Prior to launching into the main topics in this book, let's step back and think about some of the core assumptions of a work that calls itself *Java: The Good Parts*. As a colleague of mine was wont to say, "good" is such a value-laden term that it is proper to first think about what we mean when we say that a programming language, or part of a programming language, is good.

What makes a programming language good, and what parts of a language contribute to the goodness of the language, is generally a debate best undertaken late at night with the aid of considerable chemistry. Such debates—and they are always debates, never simple discussions—have a certain nonterminating nature to them, much like debates over the best editor, the proper way to format code, or open source licenses. In an attempt to keep my mailbox from overflowing on the date of publication of this book (or, perhaps, on the date that the book is first read), it may be worthwhile to look for a moment at the notion of "best" or "good" with regard to a programming language.

The most famous (or infamous) seed for such discussions is Richard Gabriel's essay *The Rise of "Worse is Better."* In this essay, Gabriel gives a convincing argument that Lisp was (and is) a better language than C, but that C won anyway because of all sorts of factors that had nothing to do with the goodness of the languages. In fact, according to the essay, it was because C and Unix were worse than their alternatives (Lisp and Multix) that those languages were able to come to dominate programming.

The main problem with the argument (which I've pointed out before)[†] is that it makes the mistake of thinking that "worse" and "better" are predicates denoting properties that adhere to entities directly.[‡] Put more simply, these discussions assume that you can talk about a language being good or bad in a vacuum, or in some absolute fashion.

---

[*] There are a number of versions of this essay, but the one I usually refer to is *http://www.jwz.org/doc/worse-is-better.html*.

[†] See *http://www.artima.com/weblogs/viewpost.jsp?thread=24807*.

[‡] In rereading this, I realize that the time I misspent as a youth studying philosophy is showing itself. Please bear with me; this won't last long.

But that's the wrong way to think about these notions, especially when applying them to things that are means to some other end. One shouldn't argue or even assert that programming language x is better than programming language y, because "better than" requires a third term. We need to know what you are trying to do with the programming languages before you can talk about which one is better than the other. Likewise, if you want to talk about a language being worse or better, you have to say what you are using them for. A language is worse or better at doing some things, and for different things, you may get a different answer on which language is worse or better.

To see why this matters, let's go back to Gabriel's *Worse is Better* argument. What Gabriel showed was that Lisp was simpler, allowed the programmer more flexibility, was surrounded by a better set of programming tools, and was better for rapid development of code. What he didn't point out is that C, at the time, was available on much cheaper hardware, and code written in the language ran much faster (on the cheap hardware) than code written in Lisp. The fact that C won the language battle didn't so much show that something worse was valued more than something that was better, but that the people making the decisions valued the places where C was better more than they valued the places that Lisp was better.

What Gabriel presupposed in his argument was that the factor that made a programming language good was the productivity of the individual programmer using that language. Even if we buy all of his arguments, the best we could conclude is that Lisp was a better programming language for an individual programmer. But that aspect of the language had to be balanced against the cost of the environment, where the C language was better. It wasn't that C was worse; it was that it was worse for some things and better in others. The reason that C won the programming language war was that running fast on cheap hardware was more important to those making the decisions (who, generally, were not programmers) than increased individual programmer productivity.

The relevance of all this to the current book is that, before I can launch into talking about the good parts of Java, I need to spend a little time talking about what Java is good for. I'm not going to claim that the parts of Java I'm going to talk about in what follows are always the good parts, no matter what you are trying to do with the language. Nor am I going to try to claim that Java itself is the language you should use for any and all of your programming needs. Java is a tool, and any craftsman[§] who relies on a single tool is going to have a hard time with some jobs. Perhaps everything you do is the kind of thing where Java is the appropriate tool. But if you have a programming task where some other language is more appropriate than Java (and there are lots of such tasks), then citing that task as something that Java does badly does not mean that Java is not a good language. It just means that Java isn't good for that task.

[§] Yes, this assumes that programming is a craft. I've argued this elsewhere (see *http://research.sun.com/techrep/Perspectives/PS-2006-6.pdf*) and so won't rehash the argument here.

What Is Java Good For?

So what is the Java language good for? Or, more precisely, what are the situations in which I find myself reaching for the tool that is Java?

First, I find Java a useful tool when I'm working on a project that is either so large, so complex, or on such a short schedule that I need to be working with other programmers to get it done. Java has a number of characteristics that allow you to break the work up into smaller, independent pieces, and then ensure that those pieces really stay independent. There are also features of the language that make it easier to explain to others what you are doing and how the system fits together, which also aid in this sort of multiperson effort.

I find the Java language and environment to be a useful tool when the code that I am writing needs to run on multiple platforms. The claim that you can write your code once and run it anywhere with the Java language and the Java virtual machine is, to a large extent, true. It has been bashed for a number of reasons, some of them absolutely true, but most of which have to do with the graphics libraries or the look-and-feel of the user interface. These are hard problems, and it isn't even clear what the right answer is with respect to some of them. I remember debates in the Java organization about whether "write once, run anywhere" meant that the user interface would look the same on all platforms, or meant that the user interface would look like the native interface on the platform, a problem especially vexing if you support both Windows and Mac. It is also true that running everywhere does not always mean running *optimally* everywhere. For real performance-sensitive applications, some tuning might be needed.

But for the most part, Java bytecodes will run the same on the Java virtual machine no matter what the platform. And this is certainly a far cry from the kind of "portable" C or C++ code that we've had in the past, where "portability" meant that you could compile most or all of the code on any machine (after running the appropriate configuration files), and then start debugging once the compile completed successfully. Java's notion of portability has to do with the object code, and if there is any debugging to be done, it is the responsibility of the virtual machine vendor, not the application writer. Having a portable binary format is a different sort of thing, and a real advantage if you are going to run on multiple machines.

Java is a useful tool when the code you are writing is going to be used for a long time, either by itself or as a component or library that is designed to have lots of different users. There are complexities with getting a Java program started, and there are complexities that make Java an inconvenient choice for a one-off, quick hack, or experimental program. In fact, I would venture to say that Java is best used on systems that are designed before they are written (at least to some level of exactitude) rather than those that grow as the code is produced.

Finally, I would say that Java is a useful tool if the code you are writing needs to be reliable. Of course, all of us write programs that are meant to be reliable. But there is a trade-off between the kinds of freedoms we can have in writing our code and the reliability that the language and environment force on us. The Java language and environment have made a number of design decisions that are meant to make the code written more reliable, even if it makes the programmer's experience somewhat more difficult.

So when, in this book, I talk about the good parts of Java, I'm going to be talking about the parts that aid in writing programs (or parts of programs) in environments in which Java itself is the appropriate choice of programming language and environment. I'm assuming that you are using Java for a large, multiperson project that is producing long-lived programs or components that need to be highly reliable, and that those programs or components will be used and modified by even more people. This is not all of programming, and for other kinds of programming activities in other kinds of environments, what I will be talking about might not make Java a good language, and in fact Java itself might be the wrong tool for the job. For clarity of exposition, in what follows, I will talk about things that are good parts of Java. When I do, you should understand that I mean "good part of Java, for doing the things that Java is good for doing."

When I first started using Java, one of the real attractions of the language and the environment was the simplicity of it all. There was a language that generated bytecodes that would run on any Java virtual machine, no matter what the underlying operating system. There were a small number of libraries that provided basic functionality, all written by the same small group of engineers and all sharing a similar design philosophy. If you knew C or C++, Java was easy to learn. Although some libraries may have been better than others, they were all reasonable.

Since then, Java and the associated environment have grown tremendously, both in popularity and in size. Java started out as a language for writing web applications that would run in a browser, and is now a language that is used for core system programming in the enterprise. The language itself has seen a number of major and minor additions, ranging from generic types (major) to autoboxing (minor). The platform has grown from a single entity to multiple editions, from Java Enterprise Edition and Standard Edition to all of the small Java environments for phones and smart cards. The set of libraries has grown at an even faster rate.

The end result is an overall system that has grown in complexity and can be daunting to those trying to master it. But within this large and complex system, there is still the small and simple core system, if you just know where to find it. The goal of this book is to show that small, simple system that every Java programmer who is using Java for what the language and environment are good for should know. This is not meant as a tutorial in the language; there are many of those, so I'm going to assume that you are familiar with Java and can read the examples without a lot of explanation. Nor is this an attempt to show you the clever tricks and techniques that will allow you go get the most out of your Java program—others have done that job far better than I can do it.

Instead, this is a reminder of which parts of the language are useful in all situations, and at times, a reflection on why particular design choices were made or not made. My hope is that you will come away from this book with a reinforced view of the use of certain parts of the language, and a better understanding of why those parts of the language are useful, when to use them, and when to avoid other solutions. Along the way, there will be some digressions on the history of the language and environment, along with unjustified (but not, I hope, unjustifiable) opinions on the art of program-ming, system building, and software design. There will be times, no doubt, that the text veers from description of the language and becomes unintentionally confessional, in that the viewpoints might tell the reader more about the author than about the right way to do things in Java. When that happens, all I can say is that there is no right way to do things in Java (or any other language), but these are ways that have worked for me. And they may help you avoid the many wrong ways of doing things, which is no small thing in itself.

If nothing else, I can say that what follows are some discussions of the features of Java that I have found useful in my work over the past 15+ years. I do mostly system (more precisely, distributed systems) programming, so there is very little about building graphical user interfaces in what follows. I don't do beans, or enterprise applications, so most of Java Enterprise Edition is ignored. This is more a reflection of my experience than a reflection of those parts of the Java environment. The fact that something isn't discussed in this book may not mean that it isn't a good part of Java, but rather that it is a part of Java that I haven't had to use.

This is not to say that all of Java is good. There will be times in what follows that I will talk about things that should be avoided, or that seemed like a good idea at the time but have since turned out to be, well...less than good ideas. Some of these are ideas that I helped bring into the language, so I'm not going to try to assign praise or blame. But one can't talk about the good without contrasting it with the bad. At least I can't, and I haven't tried here.

CHAPTER 2

The Type System

If I had to pick a single best part of the Java programming language, it would be the type system. Like many other parts of the language, there is nothing new to the type system. Every object is an instance of a type, and those types are determined by the class of the object and the interfaces that the class implements. An object actually is an instance of many types (hence the notion of a *polymorphic* type system). This polymorphic aspect of objects allows many of the patterns that have become so popular to work, as we can write code that uses the properties of objects of one type and then manipulate objects that are at least of that type (but may also be an instance of some other type). After working with the Java language for more than a decade, we tend to take the type system for granted, or worse yet, notice it only when it gets in the way. But if we think about it, the type system in Java is a paradigmatic example of what makes the language what it is—a pragmatic combination of features that provide an excellent tool for software engineers building large, complex systems.

The Basics

The basics of the type system are simple to explain (which by itself is a positive feature). Every object in a Java program is an instance of a *class*. The class defines the internal data layout for the object and defines a set of *methods* that can be called on the object. The class also associates code with each of these methods, allowing that code to manipulate the data in the object. A class can *extend* another class, in which case it *inherits* all of the data and methods of the class that it extends. A class also inherits the implementations of the methods of a class it extends, or a new implementation can be supplied that *overrides* the inherited implementation. The relationship of extending forms a tree in which all classes can be located. The root of that tree is the class Object, which all other classes extend (either directly or indirectly).

In Java, a class may extend only one other class. This means that Java is a single-inheritance language, at least as far as the types defined by classes are concerned. This might not be as great a limitation as some have thought. Arguments have been put forward that anything that can be done with multiple inheritance can be done just as well (and without the complexity of multiple inheritance) using single inheritance and delegation.[*] Having only single inheritance at the level of the class (which is to say, at the level of the actual implementation of the type) simplifies not only the language but the job of the programmers, since it makes it easy to find the code that is being run when you call some method. If the method has been overridden, you can find the code in the code for the class itself. If the method has not been overridden, you can look at the most direct parent of the class and apply the same search strategy. There are no inheritance diamonds where you need to check two possible implementation paths. But this doesn't mean that there is no notion of multiple inheritance in Java. That notion is supplied with the other aspect of the type system.

This other part of the type system is the *interface*, which allows the declaration of a set of methods that must be implemented as a unit by any class that states that it implements the interface. A class can implement any number of interfaces, and any class that extends another class must implement all of the interfaces that are implemented by the class that it extends (although it can also implement other interfaces). Like a class, an interface defines a type, and an object that is an instance of a class that implements an interface is an instance of that interface type as well. Since a class can implement multiple interfaces, the set of interfaces does not necessarily form a tree but at best a directed graph (and, more generally, a lattice), and there is no single root to that graph. By themselves, interfaces cannot be instantiated into objects, but parameters and return values can be declared as interfaces. Only classes can be directly instantiated.

Somewhere in the ontological middle between classes and interfaces are *abstract* classes. These are like standard classes in that they allow one to describe an associated collection of data, and to define a set of methods on that data, and even implement some of those methods. But like interfaces, abstract classes also allow a method to be defined that has no implementation. The goal is to allow the implementation in classes that extend the abstract class. Like interfaces, abstract classes cannot be directly instantiated into objects. But like classes, only a single abstract class can be extended by another class; abstract classes form part of the single-inheritance tree of classes.

This is the core (and, during the first years of the Java language, the only) mechanism for defining a type in the Java language. But that is only part of the story of the type system. The other part is how types get used in the language.

Historically, types have been used in computer languages to allow the compiler to determine the amount of space to allocate for objects of the associated type. This is relevant only for the types in the Java language that are defined by classes, since only classes can have instances that need space allocated for them. Types are also used to describe arguments and return values for methods, allowing the compiler or the run-time system to know the sizes of those entities as well. If these were the only reason for types in the Java environment, there would be no use for interfaces. Interfaces play into

---

[*] One example of this argument is given by Thomas Cargill in "Controversy: The Case Against Multiple Inheritance in C++," *Computing Surveys* Vol. 4 No. 1 (winter, 1991).

the far more important use of the type system, which is to allow compile-time checking of the arguments and return values passed to and returned from methods.

All methods in the Java language are defined by their name and by the types of their arguments (the objects that are passed in to the method) and their return values (the object, if there is one, that is handed back by the method).[†] If Foo, Bar, and Baz are all types defined in our program, then we can define a method quux as:

```
Foo quux (Bar arg1, Baz arg2)
```

This tells us that the first argument passed in to the method quux must be of type Bar, the second must be of type Baz, and the value returned will be an object (actually, a reference to an object) of type Foo. Best of all, this is something that the compiler will enforce. If we try to pass something other than a Bar into the method quux as the first argument, we will be told that the object being passed in is not of the correct type, and the compiler will refuse to compile the code. Further, if we have a method declared as:

```
Foo quux (Baz arg1, Bar arg2)
```

this will be seen as a different method than the one declared previously.

This makes the Java language type-safe; that is, it is impossible to pass (or return) an object of the wrong type to a method. Those of us who use languages such as Java or C++ are so used to this language feature that we tend to forget that there are many languages that have a type system but are not type-safe. There are languages that use types only to size objects, and allow anything to be sent into or returned from a method. Those languages allow great flexibility, but also rely on the programmer to ensure that the right things are handed to these methods. The Java compiler may trust, but it also verifies.

Why Have Three?

Having three different ways to define a type—classes, abstract classes, and interfaces—may seem excessive to some. Indeed, I have seen lots of code that never uses the **interface** keyword and does all of its work with classes and abstract classes. This was especially true in the early days of Java, when there was more worry about the efficiency of the programs that were written in the language. Declaring a type using an interface and then having that interface implemented by a class, the reasoning went, added an extra level of indirection to call the methods that were defined in the interface. The runtime performance of calling through an interface, on this view, was not something that the designers were willing to pay. But even in the early days of the Java interpreter, when acceptable performance was a real concern, this was such a minor optimization

---

† At this point, we are ignoring the exceptions that can be raised by a method. This is in part for simplicity, in part because methods in Java cannot be distinguished purely on the basis of different exception values, and in part because we will be discussing exceptions in a separate chapter.

that it didn't really make much sense. With the current performance of just-in-time compilers, this objection makes no sense at all.

A second efficiency argument that is often presented against the use of Java interfaces has to do not with the runtime efficiency of the program, but with the coding-time efficiency of the programmer. On this argument, interfaces are to be avoided because they duplicate information in the system, requiring the programmer to do more code entry and create more files. Why declare an interface, such arguments go, when all of the information about the method names, input parameters, and return values will just have to be typed again when implementing a class that implements that interface?

Such thinking misses the importance of interfaces to good systems, and shows a failure to understand how interfaces are part of what makes the type system in Java one of its best features. The interface defines an abstraction that a class implementing that interface makes concrete. Different classes may make the interface abstraction concrete in different ways, but they still have the abstraction that is captured by the interface in common. That Java has a way of expressing what these different implementations have in common is a strength of the language, not a weakness.

The need for the declaration of the methods that appear in an interface to be duplicated in the classes that implement the interface is also a strength rather than a weakness. By separating the declaration of the method signatures from the class that implements the method, the compiler can find those cases where a programmer changes the signature of a method or makes a typo in the name of the method. Further, you can trust that the other programmers on your team are using the same interface definition because all the classes that implement a particular interface will share a common definition. Even the objection that this split between defining interface and implementing class causes extra typing is mitigated by modern integrated development environments (IDEs), which will automatically insert the proper code in your class files.

It is in the declaration of the arguments and return values of a method that the notion of an interface can first be seen as important. The compiler requires that the objects passed into a method or returned from the method be of the declared type. But those objects don't need to be exactly of that type; they are required only to be of *at least* that type. If the type is one that is defined by a class, then any object that is an instance of a subclass of that class can be used. This means that you can pass a subclass into a method that is declared as taking objects of the type of the superclass. This is interesting because any method called on the object passed in will be dispatched to the code for the subclass, not the superclass, which means that new things can happen inside of old code.

As the name suggests, the real purpose of an interface is to give those who want to use an object the set of operations that can be performed on the object. Just as the user interface of a program determines how the human user can manipulate the program, the Java interface, properly defined, tells a programmer how the object can be manipulated. The interface to an object is, in fact, a user interface, but the users are programmers.

But the most important reason to use interfaces has to do with how they can clarify the overall design of a system. When properly designed, an interface defines a semantic unit, that is, a set of operations that give meaning to each other. As such, the interface should be thought of as the basic unit of meaning in a Java program or a system of such programs. This connection between the interface and meaning is generally not well understood, so we will look at an example to see what I'm talking about.

Suppose we are building a system to keep track of statistics for baseball players. We could try to keep all the information needed to generate all the possible kinds of statistics for every player in a single class, but that would be missing some knowledge about the game (and the statistics kept about the players). Instead, we will define different interfaces for the different kinds of statistics and different kinds of players.

The most commonly known baseball statistics have to do with hitting. There are lots of different statistics that we could keep on a hitter, but we will define an interface that allows us to keep track of only a few:

```java
package examples;
/**
 * An interface that defines the notion of a batter
 * in a baseball statistics package. Each at-bat will
 * be recorded for the hitter, along with the result of
 * that at-bat. Running totals of the important statistics
 * will be available.
 *
 */
public interface Batter {
    /**
     * The possible results of an at-bat for the hitter.
     *
     */
    enum AtBatResult {
        strikeOut, fieldOut, base1, base2, base3, base4, walk,
        reachOnError, sacrifice
    }
    /**
     * Return the batter's name. Note that the
     * interface does not define how the name is set;
     * this will be done when the object implementing the
     * interface is created and cannot be changed.
     * @return The name of the batter, as a string
     */
    String getName();
    /**
     * Method used to record an at-bat. The result
     * of the at-bat is passed in and recorded.
     * @param what The result of the at-bat
     */
    void atBat(AtBatResult what);
```

```
/**
    * Return the batting average for the hitter, defined as
    * number of hits divided by the number of at-bats.
    * @return The batting average, as a float
    */
float getAverage();
/**
    * Return the on-base percentage for this hitter, defined as
    * (hits + walks)/at-bats.
    * @return the on-base percentage
    */
float getOBP();
/**
    * Return the slugging percentage for the batter, defined as
    * (total number of bases)/at-bats.
    * @return The slugging percentage, as a float
    */
float getSlugging();
/**
    * Return the total number of bases for the hitter.
    * @return Total bases, as an integer
    */
int getTotalBases();
/**
    * Return the total number of at-bats for this hitter. Note that
    * walks and sacrifices do not count as at-bats.
    * @return
    */
int getAtBats();

}
```

So what, we can ask, are the semantics of the operations that we have defined in the interface? A usual response to this question would refer to the internal representation of the object that implements the interface. We would say that there are state variables in any object of a class that implements the Batter interface that hold the number of at-bats and the various results of those at-bats. But this explanation presupposes an implementation of the Batter object that might not be the actual implementation. After all, the class could have been implemented with an internal representation that calculated the number of at-bats from the sum of the various results, or calculated the various averages on the fly. One of the reasons that we use object-oriented techniques is to allow for such variation where the different implementation strategies don't change the semantics of the interface. But that means that we have a notion of the semantics of the interface that is separate from the implementation.

A far more accurate way to explain the semantics of the interface is to give the meanings of the methods in terms of each other. The meaning of getAtBats(), on this approach, is that it returns the value equivalent to the number of times the atBat() method has been called with an argument other than walk or sacrifice. The methods that return the various statistics can be explained with reference to each other or to the atBat()

method. Such descriptions not only allow you to give the semantics of a method without presupposing the implementation of that method, but also help to make sure that you are designing your interfaces correctly. If you can't describe the meaning of your interface without referring to methods of some other interface, then you have two interfaces that are dependent on each other, and that dependency should be reflected in some way. If you have to describe the semantics of the operations of an interface by referring to something in the implementation of a class, then you have an interface that depends on implementation details, and something is wrong with your design.

The side effect of explaining the semantics of a method in terms of the effect on other methods within the interface is that it gives an immediate way to write some quick tests for any class that attempts to implement that interface. For example, if we wanted to test implementations of the Batter interface, we could write a simple class like:

```java
package examples.test;

import org.junit.Test;
import examples.Batter
import examples.Batter.AtBatResults;
    /**
     * A class that checks an implementation of the Batter
     * interface. An instance of the class will be initialized with
     * an array of AtBatResult objects that will be used to generate
     * statistics in a Batter instance. The tests will then ensure
     * that the statistics reported are correct.
     * For simplicity's sake, the current implementation
     * only checks the Slugging Average.
     */
public class CheckBatter {
    private Batter.AtBatResult[] testData;

    public CheckBatter(Batter.AtBatResult[] data){
        testData = data;
    }
    @Test
    public void testGetSlugging() {

        for (int i = 0; i < testBatters.length; i++) {
            float testAvg = testBatters[i].getSlugging();
            float calcAvg = (float)testBatters[i].getTotalBases()
                    / (float)testBatters[i].getAtBats();
            assertEquals("Slugging test", testAvg, calcAvg, .02);
            }
        ...
    }
```

This simple test uses the JUnit testing framework, which will be discussed in Chapter 11. The important thing to understand is that the test creates an object that holds an array of AtBatResults instances. When passed an object that implements the Batter interface, it calls the atBat() method with the results, and checks to make sure that the slugging average, total bases, and total at-bats statistics obey the invariant that defines those statistics. This is a very simple case; the real point to this example is that the test cases follow directly from the explanation of the meaning of the methods in the interface, without needing to reference any of the internal state of the object instance of the class being tested. That Java enables this sort of abstract description and testing is one of the good parts of the language.

Now let's consider a second interface for our baseball statistics package, which we will use to keep track of fielding statistics. Fielding has no relationship to hitting, so there is no need to refer to any of the hitting statistics to explain the fielding statistics. Since we are using interfaces as the unit of meaning, we will declare a new interface to deal with this new set of statistics. Our fielding statistics interface looks like:

```
package examples;

/**
 * An interface that defines the notion of a fielder
 * in a baseball statistics package. A fielder will have
 * attempts, which will be recorded along with the results
 * of that attempt. Running statistics for the fielder
 * are then available.
 *
 */
public interface Fielder {
    /**
     * Enumeration of the possible results of a fielding
     * try. Results are either an out, an error, or an
     * assist.
     *
     */
    enum AttemptResult{
        putOut, error, assist
        }

    /**
     * Record a fielding try
     * @param what The result of the try
     */
    void fieldTry(AttemptResult what);

    /**
     * Record that an inning has been played by the fielder.
     */
    void playInning();

    /**
     * Return the fielding average, defined as (trys - errors)/trys.
     * @return A float that is the player's fielding average
     */
    float getFieldingAverage();

    /**
     * Return the player's fielding range, defined as
     * ((putouts + assists)/innings) * 9.
     * @return a float that is the fielder's range
     */
```

```
    float getRange();

    /**
     * The number of assists (total) for this player.
     * @return the assists, as an integer
     */
    int getAssists();

    /**
     * The number of fielding attempts by this player.
     * @return The attempts, as an integer
     */
    int getAttempts();

    /**
     * The number of errors committed by this player.
     * @return the number of errors, as an integer
     */
    int getErrors();

    /**
     * Return the name for this player. Note that the interface
     * does not define how the name is set; this is done when
     * an object implementing this interface is created.
     * @return the name of the player, as a String
     */
    String getName();

}
```

This interface defines a set of statistics that can be explained in terms of each other, but none of them need to refer to the statistics defined in the Batter interface. So we do have independent units of meaning, which helps to validate our design. We can further validate this separation by realizing that, while most Player objects will implement both of these interfaces, there is no necessary connection or requirement that they do. Not all batters need to be fielders (especially in the American League, but even in the National League there are players who are only pinch-hitters). Not all fielders are hitters (pitchers in the American League). More importantly, the semantics surrounding the statistics of hitting have nothing to do with the semantics of the statistics that relate to fielding. So we define the two in separate interfaces, mixing them in those implementations where both are needed, but keeping them conceptually separate in our design.

Once we start thinking this way, we see that there are a number of other relationships that we can capture in the type system. All catchers, for example, are fielders, but there are other fielding statistics we might want to track (such as passed balls) that apply only to catchers. This would lead us to a Catcher interface that extends the Fielder interface. Similarly, all pitchers are fielders, but there is a dizzying array of statistics that we would want to track for pitchers that don't apply to other fielders. Whether we want a Pitcher interface to extend the basic Fielder interface or have a separate interface just for pitching statistics (and then have the `Pitcher` class implement both of those interfaces) is a separate design decision.

The good part about Java's type system is that the separation between interface and class allows us to do our semantic design (which has to do with interfaces) separately from our class design (which has to do with implementations). Such a separation allows us to think about the meaning without thinking about how we are going to implement that meaning, simplifying both tasks.

Inside and Out

This leads us back to why it is important to declare arguments and return values using interfaces rather than classes. When you pass in an object to a method, all that the code in the method should care about is the set of operations that can be performed on that object. How the method is implemented should never be assumed by the method that receives the object, because that can always change. In fact, all that the method should care about are the relations between the various methods for the objects that are passed in. And this is what is defined by the interface, not the class.

Similarly, all the recipient of a return value object should have to know about that object is the set of operations that can be performed on it. There is no need to know how those operations are implemented or the actual state that is stored in the object. There may even be other operations on the object that are not relevant to the receiver. All that needs to be known is the interface of the object returned.

This gives us a guideline for good use of the Java type system. Interfaces are used to define sets of interrelated operations that, taken together, form a unit of meaning in an application. An interface tells us a minimum of what an object does, and is the way to define arguments and return values for a method. Methods require as arguments objects that do at least what the interfaces specify, and methods return an object that does at least what the interface specified as the return value requires.

Classes, on the other hand, allow us to define a set of related data, and to associate that data with the code that is used to manipulate that data. Classes really allow us to do the basic association of object-oriented programming, which is to associate some collection of data with the code that is used to manipulate that data. The association of inheritance allows us to extend both the set of data that is clustered together and the code that manipulates the data. When we extend one class with another class, we can add data to the collection that is associated, add or replace implementations of the methods that manipulate the data, or simply reuse the code that was written for the class being extended.

If we take this distinction between class and interface seriously, we end up with an overarching rule for good design. Methods will be declared in an interface, along with the other methods that, taken together, form a semantic unit. Extensions of an interface will declare methods that can refine the meaning of the original interface. The arguments and return values of these methods will all be defined in interfaces as well.

Classes will define a set of data items that can be used to store information for the particular implementation of the class (hidden, as will be discussed in a different chapter), and will specify a set of interfaces that declare the methods used to manipulate the state. A class will also contain the code that is used to implement the methods declared in the interface. This code may include additional implementation-specific "helper methods" that are not declared in the interfaces. In this way classes provide the concrete details of a particular implementation of some set of interfaces.

Is there ever a time when you want to declare the type of an argument or a return value to be a class rather than an interface? Since a class is a concrete implementation of some particular set of methods, the only time you would want to do this would be if there were only one possible way to implement those methods. There have been some times when I have believed this of a class, but in all such cases the passage of time has proved me wrong. I can only speak from my personal experience, but whenever I've declared a method to have an argument or a return value that isn't of some interface type, I have later regretted it. Your mileage may vary, but not by much. If your system is going to last, you are better off ensuring that all methods take arguments and return values declared with interfaces.

There are rare times when you might want to declare a method as part of defining a class rather than as part of an interface. This most often happens when you need to add a method or two to the objects of a class that aren't really part of the core functionality of that class and really are tied to a particular implementation. One example of this is when you want to break the implementation of an externally visible method into more manageable pieces. Another example is debugging methods, or those that allow you (the programmer) to look at parts of the internal state of the object. Even in these cases, you may find that you are adding the same collection of methods to different classes, which is a sure sign that you should have declared an interface with the methods so that you can find all of the places where the methods are used. But often expediency will get in the way of good design. These methods are the design equivalent of belching in public; you know that you shouldn't do it, but sometimes it is required.

Then, of course, there are times when you are defining some class that is internal glue to some implementation you have, or that is needed inside of some code that you didn't write but need to fix. Spending the time to build an appropriate abstraction in the form of an interface may not be needed or even justified in these conditions. Like everything else in software, there are no absolute design rules, and good design requires judgment on the part of the designer. But not defining the interface, and not using that interface in method declarations, should be the exception rather than the rule.

Beware

Although the type system in Java is a great aid in building large-scale software, there are some features of the system to avoid (we will see them in a moment), and others that are, at best, odd. We will look at one of the oddities first. This is an aspect of the type system that could trip up a design (although it rarely does).

We can see an example of what I am talking about in our baseball statistics package. In this package we have two interfaces, the `Batter` and the `Fielder` interface, that both have a method declared as:

```
String getName();
```

which is supposed to return the name of the player whose statistics are being held in the object that implements the interface. The methods have the same signature; they each take no argument and they each return a `String`. If we have some class that implements both of the interfaces, we need to know how to deal with a single method that is defined in two different interfaces.

For this case, the way the Java language works corresponds nicely to our intuitions. What the Java language says in this case is that there is really only one method to be implemented, even though it is defined in two different interfaces. The `getName()` method in the two interfaces is really the same method.

Although this works fine in this case, we can think of others where it would be more of a problem. Consider an interface for a graphical object, which defines methods to get and set the origin of the object, and one to make the object appear on the screen:

```
public interface GraphicsObject{
    Point getOrigin();
    void setOrigin(Point newOrigin);
    boolean draw(Point drawOrigin);
    ...
    }
```

Now suppose that we have a separate interface in which we define the activity of the `Cowboy` objects that are going to be part of our program:

```
public interface Cowboy {
    boolean ride(Horse toRide);
    boolean rope(Cow toRope);
    boolean draw(Point toShoot);
    ...
}
```

Our `Cowboy` objects do the usual things that cowboys do. They ride (or try to ride) horses. They rope cows. But they also get into gunfights, where they have to draw their pistols and fire at some particular point.

But now we want to build a new computer game with a Wild West theme, and we need to define a class:

```
public class GraphicalCowboy implements GraphicsObject, Cowboy {
...
}
```

As in our previous example having to do with baseball statistics, we find that we have a method with the same name and signature defined in two different interfaces that are implemented by the same class. In this case we want very different implementations for the two methods. But given the type system of Java, we can't; there is only one Draw() method, even at the GraphicalCowboy level.

This problem is caused because Java interfaces do not create a separate namespace, and hence there is no way to disambiguate the draw() that is defined in the Cowboy interface from the draw() that is defined in the GraphicsObject interface. The methods have the same name, take the same argument, and return the same value. So from the Java point of view, they must be the same.[‡] It doesn't have to be this way. It would have been possible to define Java interfaces so that they created their own namespace, and we could distinguish between GraphicalObject.draw() and Cowboy.draw() in the same way that we can use packages to distinguish between classes or interfaces that have the same name. It would mean that when you were implementing a class that has two methods from different interfaces with the same name and you want to share the implementation, you would need to implement one by making a call to the other, which creates its own set of headaches. But Java isn't that way, and making the change now could result in breaking a lot of existing code, so it will probably never be that way.

This sort of example warrants only a warning because it rarely, if ever, becomes a problem in actual systems. I don't think that I have ever encountered this problem in the wild. This does mean that you should try to have descriptive names for your methods when you define an interface, and should think of other meanings of those method names that could result in some other interface using the same name (and method signature) for a method with a very different semantics. Method names such as method1() or doIt() should be avoided, for this reason and many others.[§] But if you are building a large system with methods named like that, then the equivalence of such methods in different interfaces may be low down in your list of worries.

A Real Problem

Whereas the lack of different namespaces in different interfaces is a potential problem that hardly ever surfaces, the type system in Java does have one characteristic that will eventually bite just about everyone doing a large system in the language. And it all started out so simply, and with such good intentions.

[‡] Ted Goldstein, late of Sun Labs and then of Apple Computer, first described this particular example of the general problem of undifferentiated method names in interfaces to me.

[§] This could actually lead to a notion of the tragedy of the common namespace. If no one uses names like this, it is fine for you to do it. But if anyone else does, you shouldn't. But there are other reasons that you shouldn't, so don't.

Java was originally the way to provide active content on the World Wide Web. Applets, a particular kind of Java object that was recognized by browsers, could be sent from one website to the browser to animate, compute, or otherwise enliven what until then had been static content from the Web. The reason people were willing to allow such applets into their browser was that the applets (and Java in general) were billed as secure. The Java language made it difficult to write badly behaved viruses, the Java security model kept the applets from grabbing local resources, and the isolation provided by the Java object system kept different applets from interfering with each other. It is hard to remember that Java, now thought of as a heavyweight enterprise environment, started its life (and gained its original popularity) as a lightweight, secure environment to enliven web pages.

But as Java's popularity was skyrocketing, a security flaw was found. Java allows **static** fields in classes, which are shared among all members of the class. This allowed a backdoor mechanism for applets to communicate with each other. If two applets were members of a class that shared a static variable, they could use that static variable to exchange information between themselves. Thinking about this now, it doesn't seem like all that serious a security problem. But at the time, it was seen as a crack in the Java security facade, and it needed to be fixed quickly without breaking the code that already existed out in the world.

Here is how the problem was fixed. All Java classes get loaded by a classloader, which is a part of the virtual machine that brings in the bytecodes for a class and dynamically links in that class. So the first part of the fix was to make sure that each applet was loaded by a different classloader; the actual restriction was that classes coming from different locations on the Internet had to be loaded by different classloaders. So an applet that came from one website would need to be loaded using a different classloader than an applet that came from a different website. On top of this, the runtime type of an object was redefined to be the combination of the compile-time type (that is, the combination of the class and the interfaces implemented by the class) and the classloader. Since applets from different web pages would be loaded by different classloaders, they would be considered by the runtime system to be of different types, even if they had the same compile-time type. Since they were of different runtime types, they wouldn't share static fields, so the backdoor communication that led to the security worry would be eliminated. The solution worked, would not break any code that was not relying on insecure features, and was reasonably easy to implement.

But it also meant that there was now a difference between the definitions of the compile-time type of an object and the runtime type of that object. Usually this doesn't matter. If you are not loading objects over the network (more on that later) or introducing your own classloaders (which is becoming more common as people decide that classloaders are a hook for all sorts of things), two objects that have the same compile-time type will be of the same runtime type. But God have mercy on your soul if you ever have a program or system where you cross classloader boundaries. Sometimes you won't notice (because the types you are passing across the boundary are actually first defined in a common parent classloader). But when you do, you will be told that the type of an object that you are using is incompatible with the declared type, even though the source code says that they are the same. Good luck in finding the problem; even more luck will be needed to fix the problem (which generally requires introducing more class-loaders, making it even more likely that another problem like this will pop up).

Still, the type system of the Java language overall is a great way to help you design, implement, and maintain a system. It gives a structure for describing the outside of an object, and a separate way for constructing the inside. It lets the compiler tell you when things are out of whack. And it gives you a way of building units of meaning that can be shared, extended, and explained. It could be better, but as it is, it's pretty good.

CHAPTER 3

Exceptions

Few features of the Java language are as generally reviled and misunderstood as Java exceptions. Exceptions have to be declared as part of the signature of a method, and if an exception is declared as being thrown by a method, any code calling that method either needs to throw that same exception or needs to occur within a `try` block, and the calling method must include code that will `catch` the exception and deal with it. There are large numbers of programmers who hate this "extra" work and think that it makes their code messy and hard to read. Worse yet, they have to think about what could go wrong, and wrap their code calling anything that could throw an exception in a block. These blocks are uninteresting, and make it hard to remember what it is that the method is trying to do in the first place.

But exceptions in the Java language are definitely part of the good things about the language. Using exceptions correctly, your code can be easier to read. Using exceptions, your code can be more reliable. Using exceptions, your code can be easier to maintain. Those who object to the exception mechanism either don't understand it, don't realize what it can do, or are simply lazy twits who don't care about writing reliable code.* In spite of evidence to the contrary, I like to think that there are very few in the third category. So in this chapter we will talk about exceptions for those in the first two groups, explaining how exceptions should be used and why this sort of use makes them contributors to the good parts of the Java language.

---

* Actually, there are two other possible reasons that a programmer might not use exceptions. There are applications that simply can't tolerate exceptions, such as industrial control applications that deal with any failure at the very highest level of the code. There are also libraries where you can assume those who are calling the library will take care of all exceptional conditions. The first of these is rare, and the second requires a level of trust that also makes it uncommon.

The Basics

In Java, an Exception (and its evil, but necessary, twin the RuntimeException) is a class that extends the Throwable class. Anything that is an instance of a Throwable can be returned from a method by using the throw statement, and these throw return values can be caught by an exception handler in the calling method. All of which sounds complicated. An easier way to think of this is that it is possible to have a set of alternate return values in any Java method, as long as those return values are of the Throwable class (or any class that has Throwable as an ancestor class). Not only can the method in which the exception occurs return an alternate value, the calling method can indicate where processing will resume when such a value is returned.

Let's take a look at a quick example. Suppose that we have implemented our baseball statistics package from Chapter 2. But when we start working on the implementation of calculating the batting average for a player, we realize that the average is meaningless unless there are a sufficient number of at-bats. If someone asks for the average of a player with fewer than the minimum number, we don't want to return an average; instead, we will return an exception that will indicate that this mistake has taken place. The resulting code might look something like:

```java
package examples;

public class BatterImpl implements Batter {
    private int atBats;
    private int hits;
    ...
    public float getAverage() throws NotEnoughAtBatsException {
        if (atBats < 10) {
            throw new NotEnoughAtBatsException("Insufficient at bats",
                    10 - atBats);
        }
        return ((float)hits / (float)atBats);
    }
}
```

The usual return value of the getAverage() method is the number of hits divided by the number of at-bats. But if the batter in question has fewer than 10 at-bats, we send a different answer. In such a case, we throw an exception (in this case the NotEnoughAt BatsException) that is a different kind of object than the float that is returned in the usual case.

The object that is thrown when the number of at-bats is less than 10 would be an instance of a class something like:

```java
package examples;

public class NotEnoughAtBatsException extends Exception {
    private static final long serialVersionUID = 1L;
    private int atBatsNeeded;

    publicNotEnoughAtBatsException(String message, int currentBats) {
```

```
            super(message);
            atBatsNeeded = currentBats;
        }

        int getNeeded(){
            return atBatsNeeded;
        }
        ...
    }
```

The important part is that the class that defines this kind of object extends the basic class `java.lang.Exception`, which in turn extends the class `java.lang.Throwable`. We declare a `serialVersionUID` because the basic class of `Throwable` extends the `Serializable` interface, and all good classes that extend that interface will declare a `serialVersionUID` (this will be discussed fully in Chapter 9). The base class of `Throwable` contains a lot of information about the context in which the exception object was thrown. For example, a full stack trace is contained in that object, allowing the receiver of the object to find out the state of the virtual machine when the exception was thrown. This can be an immensely valuable piece of information when debugging, since it will give you the call history that led to the exception being thrown.

The receiver of an object that is returned from a `throw` is, naturally enough, a `catch` clause. In the method that called the `getAverage()` method, the call needs to be wrapped in a `try` clause that contains a `catch` of the exception. An example of this is code that looks something like:

```
    BatterImpl someBatter;
    float avg;
    ...
    try{
        ...
        avg = someBatter.getAverage();
        ...
    } catch (NotEnoughAtBatsException e){
        avg = 0;
        printf(e.getNeeded() +
            "more at bats needed for meaningful average\n");
    }
```

In this code, the call to the `getAverage()` method occurs with a `try` block. Such a block is followed by a series of `catch` clauses, each of which catches an `Exception` of a declared type. The catch of the `NotEnoughAtBatsException` indicates the place where processing in the calling function will resume if `getAverage()` throws the exception, and the variable e will refer to the exception object. If the `getAverage()` method returns normally, then the code within the `catch` clause will not be executed.

So how did the caller of the `getAverage()` method know to wrap the method in a `try` and have a `catch` for the `NotEnoughAtBatsException`? On the original design of exceptions in Java (that is, the design that was seen in the 0.9 version of the language), the caller would just have to know. If the caller failed to `catch` a thrown exception, then the next method in the call stack would be checked to see whether there was a `catch` of the thrown exception. If all of the methods in the call stack failed to catch the exception, the program would fall over in a pile of bits. This isn't as odd as it seems; it is just the sort of exception mechanism used in the C++ language.

But this didn't last when the first official release of the language (and the virtual machine) came out. As of Java 1.0, the code shown earlier for getAverage(), which had no throws clause in the declaration, wouldn't compile. At that release, the exception mechanism was changed so that any exception thrown by a method needed to be declared as part of the signature of that exception. After all, if Java is really a type-safe language, then all the types that are possible to return from a method should be part of that method's signature, and the compiler should make sure that the calling code handles the returned type. Since a thrown exception can be thought of as an alternate return value, it needs to be part of the signature.

So for the example code to actually compile, we would need to go back to the Batter interface and change the declaration of the getAverage() method to:

```
float getAverage() throws NotEnoughAtBatsException;
```

Any exception that is thrown by a method must be declared as part of the signature of that method. This tells the caller that it is possible that the exception may be thrown. In response, the caller of such a method must have a catch clause that handles the exceptions that are thrown.

The polymorphic nature of the Java type system comes into play here. If a method declares that it can throw an exception of a particular class, that method may also throw an exception of any subclass of that declared class. Similarly, if a catch clause is declared for an exception of some type, it will also catch any thrown exception that is a subtype of the declared exception type.

Declaring that a method throws a particular type of exception tells the callers of the method that the exception might be thrown. But it also tells the Java compiler that the exception can be thrown, so the compiler can enforce the rule that any method calling the exception must deal with the exception. There are two ways that the calling method can do this. The first is the one we saw earlier, where there is a catch clause that will be the point of return when the exception is thrown, and where code can be written that deals with the problem reflected in the exception. But sometimes that isn't possible, so the calling method can also declare that it throws the exception, in which case the exception is propagated up the stack to the method that called it (which in turn will be forced by the compiler to either deal with the exception or declare it as a possible exception that can be thrown). Note that it isn't turtles all the way down (or, more accurately, exceptions all the way up). Every Java program needs to start with a method that has the signature:

```
public static void main(String[] args)
```

which, you will notice, throws no exceptions. Of course, you can add exceptions to this declaration, in which case the exceptions will go all the way up.

While we have explained exceptions as alternate return values that reenter the calling method at a different spot than from where the method was called, it would be a very bad idea to literally use them in that way. Sure, you could wrap any kind of object in an `Exception`, `throw` the exception, and then grab the contained object from the `Exception` object and use it as a return value. Fortunately, I have never seen anyone actually do this. And while you could do it, it would be wrong, if for no other reason than that the performance would be terrible. Throwing an `Exception` is meant to happen when things are going badly wrong. As such, there is no reason to make the code that does the throw particularly fast. The construction of a `Throwable` requires getting a lot of state from the machine, so there is a lot of additional overhead as well.

But mostly you shouldn't do this because it is an abuse of the feature, using it in a way in which it was never intended to be used. Anyone looking at your code will wonder what you are doing, and understanding the code will be that much harder. Since the whole purpose of Java is to aid in writing large-scale systems that can be understood and maintained over time, using a trick like this defeats the purpose of the language. Knowing that you could do it might be useful at a bar, but actually doing it should be avoided.

The Why

The reasoning behind the exception mechanism in Java is pretty simple. Bad things can happen, even to good programs. When such a bad thing happens, there is a need to react to it, either by figuring out some other way to accomplish what was trying to be done when the bad thing happened, by cleaning up and gracefully exiting, or by aborting the operation in which the bad thing happened and trying something else. But the code that deals with the problem shouldn't be mixed in with the code that is used when bad things don't happen, or the program can rapidly become unreadable. In addition, programmers are probably better off if they have to deal with problems as close as possible to the time and place that they occur.

The design also ties into the Java type system. Since an exception is an alternative return value, it forms part of the signature of the method. Not declaring an exception would be like not having to declare the type of the return value. It would be very difficult to write predictable code in such a situation, and it would be difficult for the compiler to help you find mistakes.

Finally, the exception mechanism allows a program to separate the mainline code and the error-handling code. Those of us who grew up in the C or C++ tradition of coding (especially early C++, before exceptions were introduced there) are familiar with code that looked something like:

```
returnValue = makeCall(somearg1, somearg2);
if (returnValue == someImpossibleValue) {
    //take care of the error
}
```

```
returnValue1 = makeAnotherCall(somearg3);
if (returnValue1 == someOtherImpossibleValue){
    //More error code
}
...
```

This leads to some interesting challenges when one wants to write clear code. The obvious one is that the error-handling code interrupts the flow of the main code. After every call to some function or method in which something bad can happen, the code first has to check whether everything is OK and, if not, do something in response. The flow of the code is broken, and when there is a common way to respond to some problem, a lot of code is duplicated (even if the duplication is to call the same function that does the error handling).

Even worse, this approach requires that we mix in the return of standard values for a function or method with the return values that mark an error. In C, the standard was to hand back a null value when a pointer was expected, a −1 if a positive number was expected, a 0 if either a positive or negative number was expected, and...well, you get the picture. The idea that there is an "impossible" value that can be used to indicate an error is not only error-prone in itself, but also assumes that the value that is returned will never in the future become a non-error return value. Good luck, by the way, in finding all of the places that the return value is tested if you ever increase the range of the possible return values. The way out of this was to return a Boolean from the function indicating whether an error had occurred, and to have any other returned values passed back as a side effect on one of the arguments that was handed in. This approach is so common that we no longer have the strong gag reaction that it ought to cause, and instead see it as a normal way of doing things.

The idea behind the Java exception mechanism is that the error handling should be separated in the flow of the code from the mainline, non-error code, and that the way to indicate an error should be explicit rather than built into some convention on what is returned. The return value of a method should be the result of that method's natural and error-free completion. If an error occurs, that code should be placed elsewhere, associated with an object that can be used to tell you what the error was (and, if necessary, tell you more information about the error).

The other notion at the bottom of the Java exception mechanism is that the closer you are to the point at which the problem occurred, the more likely you are able to do something sensible about it. We don't expect the code that is throwing the exception to be able to deal with the problem (if it could, it shouldn't be throwing the exception). But the recipient of that thrown exception should have to deal with it, or explicitly state that they expect someone farther up the call stack to deal with it by declaring that they will be throwing the exception as well.

Well, there is one other reason for the design, but it is less often discussed. Programmers tend to be, if not lazy, at least over-committed. Writing a large system with a lot of programs made up of lots of classes and interfaces is hard, even if all you have to do is worry about the things that the programs and classes and interfaces are doing when everything is going right. If you add in the requirement that the programmer has to think about all the ways that things could go wrong, and then actually write code to deal with those problems, the task becomes much more difficult and much more complex. The Java exception design is the way it is in part to make it easier to deal with these problems. But it is also the way it is in part to ensure that if a programmer ignores these problems, he does so consciously. If you want to ignore exceptions, you have to do so explicitly; just hoping that they never happen won't be accepted by the compiler. Long experience shows that in a crunch, the only way to make a programmer do the right thing is to not generate code if he does the wrong thing.

How It Works

To see how this really works, let's revisit our baseball statistics package that we started in Chapter 2. This seems like a simple package, so why would we worry about exceptions? We push the hits and at-bats into the objects, get the statistics out, and that's it.

Except that we wouldn't want to have baseball statistics for players who had appeared only a time or two. For statistics to make sense, there must be a floor on when you start to calculate those statistics. Concentrating on the batting statistics, for example, we might decide that a minimum of 10 at-bats need to be recorded by a player before we want to count any statistics about the batting of that player. Otherwise, we will simply say that the player has not done enough to get an answer when asked about, say, his batting average or on-base percentage.

To do this, we first have to define an exception that can be thrown when a player's statistics are invalid. Earlier we saw a sketch of the `NotEnoughAtBatsException` class; now we will look at one that we might actually use (in this case, adding the needed Javadoc):

```java
package examples;

/**
 * Exception thrown when a batter has not had enough attempts to make
 * the batting statistics valid. The exception contains both a string
 * indicating the reason for the exception, and the number of additional
 * at-bats a player needs before the particular statistic is considered
 * valid.
 *
 */
public class NotEnoughAtBatsException extends Exception {
    static final long serialVersionUID = 1;
    private int atBatsNeeded;
```

```
/**
 * Basic constructor, taking the reason and the number of
 * additional at-bats needed for a statistic to be valid
 * @param message
 * @param needed
 */
public NotEnoughAtBatsException(String message, int needed) {
    super(message);
    atBatsNeeded = needed;
}

/**
 * Returns the number of at-bats needed for this exception to
 * not be thrown for this batter.
 * @return an integer showing the number of additional at-bats
 * needed
 */
public int getNeeded(){
    return atBatsNeeded;
}
}
```

Now we need to change our **Batter** interface to use the exception. Not all of the methods in that interface need to be declared to throw the exception; there are some measures that are reasonable without waiting for some minimum number of at-bats. So the result looks something like:

```
package examples;
/**
 * An interface that defines the notion of a batter
 * in a baseball statistics package. Each at-bat will
 * be recorded for the hitter, along with the result of
 * that at-bat. Running totals of the important statistics
 * will be available.
 *
 */
public interface Batter {
    /**
     * The possible results of an at-bat for the hitter.
     *
     */
    enum AtBatResult {
        strikeOut, fieldOut, base1, base2, base3, base4, walk,
        reachOnError, sacrifice
    }

    /**
     * Return the name for this batter. Note that this
     * interface does not define how the name is set;
     * this will be done when the object implementing this
     * interface is created and cannot be changed.
     * @return The name of the batter, as a string
     */
    String getName();
```

```
/**
 * Method used to record an at-bat. The result
 * of the at-bat is passed in and recorded.
 * @param what The result of the at-bat
 */
void atBat(AtBatResult what);

/**
 * Returns the batting average for the hitter, defined as
 * number of hits divided by the number of at-bats.
 * @return The batting average, as a float
 * @throws NotEnoughAtBatsException if the number of at-bats is
 * insufficient to establish a meaningful average
 */
float getAverage() throws NotEnoughAtBatsException;

/**
 * Returns the on-base percentage for this hitter, defined as
 * (hits + walks)/at-bats.
 * @return the on-base percentage
 * @throws NotEnoughAtBatsException if the number of at-bats, walks,
 * and sacrifices is insufficient to establish a meaningful on-base
 * percentage
 */
float getOBP() throws NotEnoughAtBatsException;

/**
 * Return the slugging percentage for the batter, defined as
 * total number of bases / at bats.
 * @return The slugging percentage, as a float
 * @throws NotEnoughAtBatsException if the number of at-bats is
 * insufficient to establish a meaningful average
 */
float getSlugging() throws NotEnoughAtBatsException;

/**
 * Return the total number of bases for the hitter.
 * @return Total bases, as an integer
 * @throws NotEnoughAtBatsException if the number of at-bats is
 * insufficient to establish a meaningful average
 */
int getTotalBases() throws NotEnoughAtBatsException;

/**
 * Return the total number of at-bats for this hitter. Note that
 * walks and sacrifices do not count as at-bats.
 * @return
 */
int getAtBats();

}
```

This interface tells us that we can get the name of a player, get the number of times the player has been to the plate, and record an at-bat without worrying about having to deal with the new exception. But if we want to know the total bases, the average, the on-base percentage, or the slugging percentage for the player, we need to be ready to be told that the player has not been up enough to make such a statistic meaningful.

We can see the effect of this if we look at the code that we wrote to test implementations of the Batter interface. Suppose we know that the minimum number of at-bats required for meaningful statistics was 10 (if we were being really careful, we would define this in some static variable, but this is a chapter on exceptions, so we will just use a constant). Then, our test code might contain something like:

```
package examples;
...
/**
 * Test that the slugging average is calculated correctly
 * with respect to the at-bats and the total number of bases.
 * This method assumes that an array of objects of type batter
 * have been generated by the setUp method.
 */
@Test
public void testGetSlugging() {
    float testAvg; calcAvg;

    for (int i = 0; i < testBatters.length; i++){
        try{
            testAvg = testBatters[i].getSlugging();
            calcAvg = (float)testBatters[i].getTotalBases() /
                    (float)testBatters[i].getAtBats();
            Assert.assertEquals("Slugging test", testAvg, calcAvg, .02);
        } catch (NotEnoughAtBatsException e){
            Assert.assertTrue("Slugging exception",
                    (10 == (e.getNeeded() + testBatters[i].getAtBats())));
        }
    }
}
```

This code looks a lot like our earlier test code. But where that earlier test code just checked to see that the result of the call to getSlugging() was calculated correctly based on the values of getTotalBases() and getAtBats(), the new test wraps the call to getTotalBases() in a try block. If an exception is thrown, we check to make sure that the exception contains the correct number of at-bats needed with respect to the number of at-bats the player already has.

All that is left is to see how our code should throw this exception. In our class that implements the Batter interface, we might have something like:

```
package examples;

public class BatterImpl implements Batter {
    private int atBats;
    private int hits;
    private int bases;
    private int baseOnBalls;
    private int sacrifices;
```

```
    private String playerName;
    ...
    public float getSlugging() throws NotEnoughAtBatsException {
        if (atBats < 10){
            throw new NotEnoughAtBatsException("Insufficient plate appearances",
                    10 - atBats);
        }
        return ((float)bases / (float)atBats);
    }
```

In the method that calculates the slugging percentage, we first check to see whether the
number of times the player has recorded an at-bat is greater than the minimum number.
If it is greater than the minimum, we continue and make the calculation. If it is not, we
create a new NotEnoughAtBatsException object, which contains the reason for the exception and the number of at-bats needed by this player to reach the point at which
the statistic is considered meaningful. This object is then thrown back to the calling
method, which can deal with it as it wishes.

Use and Abuse

The code that we just saw catching an exception is a bit odd, but it is test code, so that's
no big surprise. In this case, the exception was in some sense expected, and what we
wanted to do was to test to make sure that the exception was thrown in the right
circumstances and make sure that the fields of the exception agreed with the data that
was held in the Batter object.

A more usual catch clause would try to deal with the exceptional condition. As we will
see in Chapter 9, there are some exceptions that can be corrected in the program,
whereas others might need to generate a new exception or raise the issue to the user.
If we were building a user interface for our baseball statistics package, for example, we
would certainly want to indicate in the batting statistics for a player when there were
insufficient at-bats for an average. But we might also want to make sure that we don't
call any of the methods that could throw the exception on a batter once it has already
been thrown; we can stop our processing of such a player early and move on to the next.

Properly used, the Java exception mechanism can allow a program to structure the
error-handling code in a different location than the mainline code. So in our code that
prints out the batting statistics for a player, we could make calls to the Batter object
and not have any error code gumming up the works as we were doing our formatting.
Instead, all of the error handling would go to the end of the try statement in the
catch clause; the resulting code would look something like:

```
    public class Formatter {
    ...
        public static void Format(Batter toFormat){
            System.out.print(toFormat.getName());
            System.out.print("\t");
            try {
                System.out.print(toFormat.getAverage());
```

```
            System.out.print("\t" +  toFormat.getOBP());
            System.out.print("\t" + toFormat.getSlugging());
            System.out.print("\t" + toFormat.getAtBats());
            System.out.println("\t" + toFormat.getTotalBases());
        } catch (NotEnoughAtBatsException e){
            System.out.println("\t" + "Not enough at-bats to be significant");
        }
    }

}
```

One common abuse of the Java exception mechanism is to use it as a more verbose variation of the C-language convention of returning an impossible value that is checked immediately after the call. On this approach, the previous code would look like:

```
public class Formatter {

    public static void Format(Batter toFormat) {
        System.out.print(toFormat.getName());
        System.out.print("\t");
        try {
            System.out.print(toFormat.getAverage());
        } catch (NotEnoughAtBatsException e) {
            System.out.println("\t" + "Not enough at-bats to be significant");
            return;
        }
        try {
            System.out.print("\t" + toFormat.getOBP());
        } catch (NotEnoughAtBatsException e) {
            System.out.println("\t" + "Not enough at-bats to be significant");
            return;
        }
        try {
            System.out.print("\t" + toFormat.getSlugging());
        } catch (NotEnoughAtBatsException e) {
            System.out.println("\t" + "Not enough at-bats to be significant");
            return;
        }
        System.out.print("\t" + toFormat.getAtBats());

        try {
            System.out.println("\t" + toFormat.getTotalBases());
        } catch (NotEnoughAtBatsException e) {
            System.out.println("\t" + "Not enough at-bats to be significant");
        }
    }
}
```

This mixes our error-handling code back in with our mainline code, and produces code that is less readable than the alternative without an exception mechanism. In our particular example, the approach is obviously missing an abstraction. This is the mistake of a puppy programmer. When you encounter such code, you should correct the writer, perhaps by rolling up a newspaper and swatting the offender. You don't really want to cause pain; you just want to make sure that this never happens again.

Of course, there are also times when this approach is needed. If the way in which you are going to respond to an exception is tied not just to the exception but to the context in which the method raising the exception was called, the style of code in which each call is wrapped in a `try catch` clause may be needed. This is a rare case, but one that does arise.

Our example was simplified because all of the methods that throw an exception throw the same exception. But this is not required to cluster a group of method calls within a particular try block. All that is required is that all of the exceptions that can be thrown by any of the methods called in the try block have a `catch` clause. It is still possible to separate the mainline code from the exception-handling code.

The one trick that can cause trouble when catching multiple exception types is making sure that you don't get crossed up by the type system. When an exception is thrown, the `catch` block used as the return point is the first one encountered that deals with exceptions of that type. But an exception is a Java object, and Java objects can have multiple types; they are not only the type they are declared to be, but also of the type of any super-types of their declared type. This means that if there is a `catch` clause for a super-type of an exception listed prior to the `catch` clause for that exception, the second `catch` clause will never be the return point when that exception is thrown. Instead, the super-type exception will be caught by the earlier clause.

An example might help here. Suppose we have an exception called `Type1Exception` and another exception called `Type2Exception`, and that `Type2Exception` extends `Type1Exception`. This is the sort of thing that can happen when one exception is a more specific instance of a more general exception. Now suppose that you have a method (call it `method1()`) that can throw a `Type1Exception`, and a method (call it `method2()`) that can throw a `Type2Exception`. If `method1()` and `method2()` both occur inside the same try block, it is important how you order the `catch` blocks associated with the `try` block. If your code looks like:

```
try{
    ...
    method1();
    ...
    method2();
    ...
} catch (Type2Exception e){
    //do something to recover
} catch (Type1Exception e) {
    //do something else to recover
}
```

the results will be as you expect. If a `Type2Exception` is thrown, the first block of recovery code will be performed; and if a `Type1Exception` is thrown, the second block of recovery code will be used instead. But if your code looks like:

```
try{
   ...
      method1();
   ...
      method2();
...
} catch (Type1Exception e){
    //do something to recover


} catch (Type2Exception e) {
    //do something else to recover
}
```

the second catch block will never be entered. That is because when an exception is thrown, it is caught by the first exception handler that matches the type of the thrown exception. Since a Type2Exception is a subclass of a Type1Exception, any Type2Exception will be caught by the first exception handler.

This sort of problem can be hard to discover when it actually happens. So when you are writing a block of code that can throw multiple exceptions, you had better take a look at all of the types (both exact and inherited) of the exceptions being thrown, and make sure that your exception handlers are declared in the correct order. You can always find such an order, since the inheritance hierarchy of any set of exceptions will form a tree rooted in the class Exception (if there were multiple class inheritance, this might not be the case). But you do need to be careful.

Of course, this advice assumes that the programmer is actually doing her job. With respect to exceptions, this often is not the case. I have heard it argued that the most common form of exception handler in Java is:

```
} catch (Exception e){
    //TODO: to be written
}
```

perhaps with the comment removed. I've not seen this, because I work with adults, but I have seen far too many exception handlers of the form:

```
} catch (SomeException e) {
    e.printStackTrace();
    System.exit(1);
}
```

Although somewhat better, this still misses the point. It is possible that the only thing you can do in the face of an exception is to print out the state of the world when the exception occurs and shut things down. But generally you can do more than that. If nothing else, there is a fair amount of cleaning up that should be done before exiting. In most specific cases, there is actually something that you can do to recover from the exceptional condition and continue with the program. All it needs is a little thought, and writing the right exception handler.

The Dark Side

What has been said thus far is true of all exceptions in the Java language. Almost. But there is an exception type that, although it is needed, can also lead to a perversion of all that is good about the Java exception system.

When the exception system was first being designed, there was worry about exceptional conditions that could occur because of problems with the machine on which the program was being run, bugs in the virtual machine, or a security violation. These sorts of things can happen at any time. But it would only clutter up the language to require that every method declare that it could throw an exception for these reasons. For one thing, it generally wouldn't be the method that throws such an exception (it would be the underlying virtual machine); for another, it would just make the code longer, not more robust.

To deal with this, a special sort of exception, the `RuntimeException`, was built into the Java environment. A `RuntimeException` can be thrown at any time, and does not need to be declared as part of the signature of a method. Further, since it can be thrown at any time, the code that might receive a thrown `RuntimeException` does not have to have a `catch` clause for those exceptions (otherwise, all code would need to be wrapped in a `try` block). This is not only for the sake of expediency, but also because there is really nothing that the application program can do to deal with the kinds of situations that are meant to be signaled by a `RuntimeException`. When one of these is thrown, the thinking went, things are so out of whack that the best thing that can happen is for the program to fall into a pile of constituent bits.

But the ability to not declare or deal with a `RuntimeException` has led to a great temptation among Java programmers. In the midst of writing the implementation of a method, a programmer discovers that there is an exceptional condition that he hadn't thought of in the original design of the system. "Make it a subclass of `RuntimeException`," a small, inner voice says. "That way you don't have to change your method declaration. All the code that calls your method won't have to be changed to deal with a new `catch` clause. Come on, no one will notice—the problem will hardly ever happen."

This is the voice of the dark side calling to you. It is the first step down the path that leads to unreliable systems. This is, not to put too fine a point on it, evil. It doesn't matter that others before you have done this, even in standard Java libraries. Resist the evil, and don't declare a new `RuntimeException`. It may be more work, but it is work that is there because it is needed. Subverting the exception mechanism is like subverting the type system (which also happens). It might make your current task easier, but it will only cause more work and heartache in the future when you try to find out why your system is failing and what method is throwing the exception that is causing everything to fall apart.

Of course, if you actually design your code to throw only subclasses of RuntimeException, then you have gone beyond simple evil. You have now become a corrupter of others, and should feel the appropriate shame and be subject to the appropriate ridicule. And you wouldn't want that, would you?

The one time that you will want to violate this principle is when you want to throw an exception that is already defined in the Java environment as a RuntimeException. For example, you may decide that you are going to require that an actual object is passed into a method, and that it is an error to pass in null instead. You could define your own Exception class for this, but there is already the exception class java.lang.IllegalArgumentException.† This exception seems to have just the right semantics for the situation in question, but it is a RuntimeException. So you are stuck between a rock and a hard place. You either throw a RuntimeException in your code, or define a new Exception class that is a duplicate of one that is defined in the platform and is in common use.

I will admit that there was a time when I was something of an Exception absolutist, and argued for the creation of a duplicate class in this circumstance. But too much water has flowed under (and, likely, over) that bridge. I still believe that the use of RuntimeException classes is a bad thing, but sometimes one needs to bow to the reality of the environment.

So now, I think that in this case the lesser of the two evils is to use the existing exception. But you should do everything in your power to warn users of your code that this exception might be thrown, the circumstances under which it will be thrown, and what the caller might to do avoid the exception or deal with it if it is thrown. It isn't the perfect solution, but it is the best that is open to you.

---

† Which preexisting exception you should throw can also be a point of contention. In this example, there are some who would prefer throwing the already-defined NullPointerException rather than an IllegalArgumentException. Since both are RuntimeExceptions, the points made here still hold. Which exception you decide to throw may be a design decision best made in consultation with your group and in a manner that is consistent through the whole group.

CHAPTER 4

Packages

One of the least appreciated good parts of Java can be found at the beginning of every Java file. This feature is so ubiquitous that most experienced Java programmers don't even notice it, much less take the time to think about what it does for them and how to use it correctly. I am speaking of the package feature of Java, along with the notion of importing from some other package. This feature, and the protection mechanisms that are part of it, is one of the simple tools that allow large-scale software to be developed in the language.

It is easy to ignore the packaging system, to use it carelessly, or to simply not give it much thought until it causes you trouble. But rightly understood, the package mechanism allows the design of the overall software system to be disentangled and made independent in a number of important ways. If your package declarations don't reflect your design decisions, you aren't using the system correctly (although you will hardly be singled out for that sin). If they do, you have introduced another mechanism to allow understanding and isolation to your system, making it easier to comprehend, develop, and maintain.

The Basics

The first bit of information that the compiler sees in any Java source file is the package declaration. There can be lots of commentary prior to this declaration (for example, it is common practice to put any licensing or copyright information in a comment at the very beginning of a source file), but the compiler discards all of that. The first thing that the compiler needs to know, and probably the first thing a programmer should think about, is the package in which the contents of the source file reside.

A package declaration is simply the keyword **package**, followed by some name, followed by a semicolon. The name of the package may be a dot-separated list of simple names, in which case a package hierarchy is being identified. For example, if the first noncomment, nonblank line in a source file is:

```
package com.sun.foo.bar;
```

you know that the code in the file is in the bar package, which is part of the foo package, which is part of the sun package, which is part of the com package.

The basic function of a package is to create a namespace. All of the names that are externally visible in a source file are scoped to that package. A name that occurs in one package can appear in a different package, and the two names will be seen as distinct. This by itself gives an independence of structure to what you are doing; as long as you are working in a different package (and namespace) than the one I am working in, we don't have to coordinate the names that we use if our work is going to be used together.

Because having separate namespaces is important, it also is important that the names of the packages themselves be different. Java is a name-equivalence language and environment, which means that things with the same name *are* the same. Thus, if I have two classes with exactly the same name but very different implementations, Java won't tell them apart; which one actually gets used will depend on the order in which the class files are encountered. Once some class with a name is loaded, any class with that same name will use the loaded implementation.[*] Making sure that your package names are unique lets you avoid unintentionally introducing a name that is the same as one introduced by someone else.

Of course, generating a unique name is not as easy as it sounds, especially if you are building some code that might be used by others at some time in the future and at some as-yet unknown place. This is really an instance of the general problem of generating unique identifiers in a distributed system (with you and all of the other programmers who use Java as nodes in the distributed system), made somewhat more complex by the lack of good connectivity between the nodes (programmers) in this particular system and the fact that the nodes are all programmed to behave in various nondeterministic ways (or, if deterministic, using an algorithm that is currently unknown). All of which is geek-speak for saying that you never know what people are going to do, and there is no way to find out until it is too late.

To help ensure that package names are in fact unique, a convention was started early in the history of Java development that a package name should start with the domain name (in reverse order) of the organization from which the package originates. Thus, packages that originate from Sun Microsystems, Inc. start with the prefix com.sun, those from Hewlett Packard, com.hp, and those from Harvard University, edu.harvard. It is up to the organization to figure out how to generate unique names, but this is a more local problem (although for these organizations, no less complex). Finally, there are some package names that are reserved for the system itself; these include the java and javax names.

---

[*] This is actually not precisely true, because of classloaders (see the discussion in Chapter 2). If we want to be completely precise, we would have to say that the two classes need to have the same name and have to be loaded by classloaders that are in the same classloader hierarchy. But this book is supposed to be about the good parts of Java, so I'm going to avoid talking about classloaders whenever possible.

Of course, there are times when I'm not writing code for any particular organization but just hacking on my own. I could, in those cases, use the same prefix as I would if I were writing for an organization. Or I could (and do) use some other string of names that make me relatively sure that the package will be unique. Email names work just fine, or personal domains. It is far more common for individuals to have network-unique names, so there is always a starting prefix that you can use for your package names.

Every source file in Java declares a package, even those that try not to. If you don't have a package declaration at the beginning of a file, the contents of that file are placed in the default unnamed package. The unnamed package is a form of namespace limbo, where code written by confused, obstinate, or lazy programmers is placed until they evolve to a higher life form. There is no good reason to place anything that you do in the unnamed package, so just say no.

Items within a single package can refer to each other by name. From another package, one way you can refer to an entity is by using the fully qualified name of the entity, which is the package name of the package the entity is in, followed by a ".", followed by the name of the entity. So if my `com.sun.foo.bar package` contains a class by the name of `baz`, I can refer to that class from outside the package using the name `com.sun.foo.bar.baz`. This is fine if I only want to refer to the class `baz` once or twice, but if I want to refer to class `baz` more often, this gets cumbersome.

The alternative is to import the name of `baz` into my current namespace. This is done, not surprisingly, by using the *import* statement. An import statement takes the form of the keyword `import`, followed by the fully qualified name that you want to import into the current namespace, followed by a semicolon. Importing the name in such a way makes it visible in the namespace of the source file, and also tells the compiler that it needs to refer (and perhaps compile) the package from which the import comes. So if I want to refer to `baz` a number of times in my source, I can include the statement:

```
import com.sun.foo.bar.baz;
```

and then I can simply use the name `baz` in my code. I could also import the entire namespace by having the statement:

```
import com.sun.foo.bar.*;
```

This would make all of the names defined in the namespace `com.sun.foo.bar` visible to this code. This more general form of the import statement is quite popular, but should be avoided if you can. By importing more than you need, you are polluting the name-space of your own code, and making it more likely that you will clash with some name that is defined in the other package. You are also introducing extra dependencies into your code. Most of the time this won't make any real difference, but when it does, it leads to problems that are hard to identify and fix. Your code is also easier for others to read if you avoid importing entire namespaces, since the reader can go to the top of a file and use the import statements to find our what package contains the imported names for the file. This advantage is somewhat minimized by the navigation functions in modern interactive development environments, but you can't yet assume that all of your colleagues use such an environment. Be nice to those who don't; they suffer enough as it is.

As a general rule, you are better off importing only those parts of another package that you really need (and that you actually refer to) rather than the whole package. Modern IDEs make this pretty straightforward, as they will import names automatically when they are used. If you really do need to import all of the names defined in another package, you might want to think about the design of your system, as you have two distinct packages that are so intertwined that you should probably only have one (or you have missed the real line that should separate the packages).

On rare occasions you will find yourself unable to import a name into a namespace. This is when that name already occurs within that namespace. Importing in such a circumstance would lead to an ambiguous name, so the name that occurs within the namespace wins. If you really need to refer to something from a different package that has the same name as something in the current package, you need to refer to the external entity using the full name (that is, with the package name as a prefix). Sometimes this can't be avoided, especially when you are using code written by someone else and he has picked all the good names.

What can be avoided is doing this to yourself. In our example, we have named our implementation of the `Batter` interface the `BatterImpl` class. But we could simply name our implementation class the `Batter` class, and say (in our source):

```
public class Batter
    implements com.oreilly.javaGoodParts.examples.statistics.Batter{
    ...
}
```

This would technically work, in the sense that it would compile. But it would also be very confusing to anyone trying to read or learn the code. It will even be confusing to you at some time in the future when you try to maintain or extend the code you originally wrote. Having separate namespaces lets you do this, but just because you can do it doesn't mean that you should.

Packages and Access Control

The package system in Java does more than just establish separate namespaces for the various parts of a system. The package system also plays into the access scheme used in the language.

Like most object-oriented languages, Java allows the programmer to declare who can access what parts (if any) of an object. As befits its C++ heritage, Java allows fields and methods to be accessed by any part of a class in which those fields and methods are declared. But outside of an object, access is defined by the access control modifier associated with the field or method. Fields or methods that are labeled `private` can be accessed only from within the defining class. Those that are labeled `protected` can be accessed either by other parts of the class or by any class that extends the defining class. Finally, those that are marked `public` may be accessed by anyone. This much is familiar to those who come to Java from C++.

But Java has an additional access category connected to the package system. Unless a field or method is marked as `private`, that field or method is also accessible to anything that resides in the same package as the field or method. This is no surprise for fields or methods that have been labeled as `public`, since anyone from any package can access such fields. But it is somewhat more surprising for those fields or methods that are marked as `protected`, since it allows access from methods that are in the package but have no relationship to the defining class through the type hierarchy. In fact, this introduces a fourth form of access specification, which is marked by there being no access specification at all. If a field or method is not labeled as being `private`, `protected`, or `public`, that field or method is said to have package access, which means that it is accessible by anything in the package, but not by anything else.

This gives a hierarchy of access possibilities for the programmer. At the most restricted are those fields and methods marked `private`, which can be accessed only from within the class in which they occur. Next most restrictive are those with no declared access specification. These have package access, which makes them available to anything that is in the same package, but keeps them from the prying eyes of anything in any other package. The next level of access, `protected`, loosens the restrictions on package protection to include any classes that are extensions of the class in which the method or field are defined, no matter where in the set of packages those extensions are defined. Finally, there are those methods and fields that are marked as `public`, which can be accessed from anywhere.

It is important to keep in mind one difference between the hierarchy formed by packages and the hierarchy formed by classes. The hierarchy formed by classes is inclusive; that is, an object that is an instance of a class is an instance of any class that is in the hierarchy above that class. This means that the protected access specifier opens the access to the field or method to any part of any class that is a continuation of the class hierarchy rooted in the class in which the method or field is declared. It is best to think of the protected access specifier as giving access to any object that is at least of the type in which the field or method is declared.

Packages, like classes, form a hierarchy that is a tree. But membership in a package is not polymorphic; that is, something that is defined in the package `foo.bar.baz` is not part of the `foo` or the `foo.bar` package. Fields and methods that have package protection can be accessed only by things that are in exactly the same package. If there is a field or method that is package protected in the package `foo.bar`, don't expect to be able to access it in the package `foo.bar.baz`.

Classes and interfaces are also subject to access specifications. However, with the exception of inner classes, the possible access specifications for these parts of the language are limited to either package access (in which case the class or interface are not labeled) or public access. A little thought convinces one that these are the only access specifiers that make sense. A class or interface that can be called only by itself is not very interesting. Neither is one that can only be called by subclasses. Although from a purely linguistic point of view, this lack of symmetry may be troubling, the fact that the language keeps you from doing something useless more than makes up for it.

You can also put some access specifications on the methods defined in an interface, but what you do here doesn't really matter. Only two access specifiers are legal for interface methods. You can mark an interface method as abstract, but doing so has no effect, since all interface methods are unimplemented at the level of the interface and are instantiated only in classes that implement the interface. Likewise, you can mark an interface method as public, but this is documentation at best; an interface method is accessible to any code that can access the interface. If the interface is marked as public, then all of the methods of that interface are public, even if that access specifier does not preface the method declaration. If the interface has only package visibility, then the methods in that interface will also have only package visibility.

An Example

Let's go back to our baseball statistics system and apply some good practice with regard to packages. We at least have a package declaration on all of our files (they are in the package examples), but it's hard to argue that the particular package name we chose is going to be globally unique. So we should probably start by picking a prefix for the package that will give us a higher confidence that the namespace for our system is unique. When I'm doing this at work, I prefix my packages with com.sun, which then only requires having a unique package among those developed within one company (the prefix, needless to say, is a lot longer; the company namespace is only the beginning). But I'm doing this work as part of a book, so I will use the prefix com.oreilly.javaGoodParts.examples.

This will ensure that the names for classes and interfaces developed within the package structure are unique (unless someone else is writing a book with the same title for the same publisher). But we are going to go further than that and start breaking apart the structure of the baseball statistics package, so that we can cluster parts that need to interact within the same package and isolate those that don't need to interact in separate packages.

The first separation we can do is between the interfaces that define the external face of the system and the implementations of those interfaces. We can place all of the interface definitions (currently, those in the files *Batter.java*, *Catcher.java*, and *Fielder.java*) in the package:

```
com.oreilly.javaGoodParts.examples.statistics
```

by starting each of these files with the line:

```
package com.oreilly.javaGoodParts.examples.statistics;
```

The implementation classes will be placed in another package. For the moment, we will only have a single implementation package:

```
com.oreilly.javaGoodParts.examples.impl
```

although that might change as the implementation gets more complex. The reason for this split is to allow clients of the basic statistics storing classes to be dependent only on the interfaces that define those classes, not on the implementation. By placing the interfaces in a separate package, we can have multiple implementations (all in their own package or packages) and the client will never be directly tied to any of them.

Splitting our code into separate packages is a form of refactoring that can ripple through our code. Now that the interfaces are in a separate package, the classes that refer to those interfaces (which are all of them) need to import the interfaces, since they are no longer in the same namespace. So along with a different package declaration, all of the implementation files will need to be changed to include an import statement. For example, our `BatterImpl` class now needs to be able to see the `Batter` interface, so we need to include the line:

```
import com.oreilly.javaGoodParts.examples.statistics.Batter;
```

for the class to compile. We could, of course, have included everything in the statistics package by replacing the import with:

```
import com.oreilly.javaGoodParts.examples.statistics.*;
```

But that would have included more than what is used in the `BatterImpl` class. I find it good practice to include only those parts of a package that are necessary. If nothing else, too long a list of imports from another package shows an interconnection between the package being imported and the package doing the importing that might indicate a design flaw. If you have to import too much from a different package, you have a lot of dependencies between them, and your package abstractions may not be correct.

The number of places that may have to be changed can get out of hand rather rapidly, especially if you are doing this kind of refactoring over a large code base. Fortunately, most modern interactive development environments (in particular, both Eclipse and Netbeans) have very good facilities that automate all or nearly all of the changes required for this kind of refactoring. This is one of the places where a good IDE really shines, although traditionalists will also be able to accomplish the same sort of thing with scripts.

An interesting question in this refactoring is where to put our exception class, `NotEnoughAtBatsException`. This is a class, as are all exceptions, and so would generally be part of the package that contains implementations. This would argue for placing it in the `com.oreilly.javaGoodParts.examples.impl` package, but the definition of the `Batter` interface in the `com.oreilly.javaGoodParts.examples.statistics` package refers to this exception. So our choice is either to import the exception from the implementation package into the interface package or to include a particular implementation in our set of interfaces.

Neither of these choices is particularly clean. The purpose of defining a set of interfaces is to allow those interfaces to be independent of the implementation classes. Importing an exception class from an implementation package explicitly ties the interface to at least part of a particular implementation. But including the exception in the interface package means that the particular implementation of the exception is part of the abstract definition of the set of interfaces, which I have argued in Chapter 2 is a bad idea.

The real cause of this problem is that exceptions in Java cannot be defined as interfaces and can be defined only as extensions of the Exception class. Since we want to declare exceptions as part of the signature of methods that are first defined in interfaces, there is no way of avoiding mixing these classes with our (more abstract) interface definitions. As language problems go, this one is actually pretty benign. Exceptions tend to be fairly simple and often carry information that is going to be needed by any implementation's exception handlers. Where you place them is more a matter of personal taste than design dictates (actually, most design dictates boil down to personal taste, which doesn't make them any less correct, but that's the subject of a different book). I prefer putting the exceptions thrown by methods defined in an interface in the same package as the interfaces, and acknowledge that (in this one case) there are implementation details that leak into the interface definitions. This means that I would be importing two items from the interface namespace when I implement the BatterImpl class, so the beginning of that class would look something like:

```
package com.oreilly.javaGoodParts.examples.impl;

import com.oreilly.javaGoodParts.examples.statistics.NotEnoughAtBatsException;
import com.oreilly.javaGoodParts.examples.statistics.Batter;

public class BatterImpl implements Batter {
    ...
```

You might choose to do things differently, and I would understand. But making use of the package system to give yourself a way of grouping interacting components of your system is a good thing about the language, so you shouldn't use the fact that exceptions keep it from being pure and perfect as a reason not to use it as part of your design. Nor should you use it as an excuse not to think about exceptions, a subject I discussed in Chapter 3.

Packages and the Filesystem

While the inability to have some packages that are implementation-independent is regrettable, the required interaction between the package system and the filesystem is both regrettable and a pain. Simply put, the interaction is that whenever you declare a component in a package name, you need to have a corresponding directory in your filesystem that corresponds to that component. This is where the compiler will look for the source files that are defined in that component, and this is where the classloaders will look for the object files that contain the binaries for the classes in those packages. Most of us who use Java have become so used to this that we don't even think about it. But it is strange and inconvenient, and has built up enough supporting cruft that it is often confusing (and the source of interesting problems, which we will see later). So I will end this chapter with some reflections on this oddity.

Just to remind you, if you have a class that begins with the line:

```
package com.oreilly.javaGoodParts.examples.impl;
```

then the source for that class will need to be in a directory (from wherever you start) with the name (on an adult operating system):

```
com/oreilly/javaGoodParts/examples/impl
```

that is, in the `impl` directory placed in the `examples` directory placed in the `javaGood Parts` directory placed in the `oreilly` directory placed in the `com` directory. At the lower level of the package naming hierarchy, this doesn't seem all that unnatural. You have different directory locations for the files that implement a related part of the system, and those parts reflect the package structure. Even at some of the higher levels this seems to make some sense; as a peer to our examples, we will have the tests for those examples, clustered in their own namespace and in their own directory.

At the next level, things get a little less sensible. I may be doing multiple books for O'Reilly, but this doesn't seem to be something that should be reflected in the filesystem on my computer. Sure, I'll keep the different books in different directories, but I might not want them to share a parent directory. And at the highest level, this just seems odd. I may be doing work for organizations that appear in different DNS domains on the Internet, but this hardly seems like a reasonable way to organize my local files.

This is where we get to see the wisdom of the adage "History clarifies stupidity."[†] What is meant by this adage is that if you understand the history of some set of decisions, you can often see why they seemed like a good idea at the time. This is the best way to understand the tie between Java packages and the filesystem.

When Java was first being implemented, there were many projects within Sun (and, no doubt, elsewhere) that were trying to build a programming environment in which the source and binary files would be kept in a database. There were lots of reasons why this would have been a good idea: it would have helped with incorporating a version control system, releases could be done more consistently, and queries over the structures held in the database could help programmers understand the structure of the system. The Java packaging system would have fit into such an environment

---

† I first heard this from my manager at the time, Mark Hodapp. I find it useful to remind myself of this fairly often, even though the initial interpretation of the adage, in which it is taken to mean that stupidity is more clearly seen in the light of history, is not the one he meant.

beautifully. The unique names would act as primary keys, and the hierarchical nature of the names would map naturally into all kinds of database structures.

But those environments weren't quite ready at the time programmers were starting to use Java widely. In fact, at the time the most common programming environments were emacs (or, inside of Sun, vi) and command lines in terminal windows. So the decision was made to use the filesystem as a cheap emulator of a database, just until the integrated environment using a real database was ready.

Of course, the integrated development environment with database never appeared. So we still use the filesystem as a database surrogate, and our package names have to be reflected in those filesystems. Fortunately, the IDEs that have appeared take much of the work out of using the filesystem in that way, doing all of the extra directory creation and transitions for us. It is less of a pain than it once was, but can still lead to confusion and lots of extra directories in the source code structure.

CHAPTER 5

Garbage Collection

So far, we have identified a number of good parts of the Java language and environment that allow us to write modular, maintainable code, often with the help (or at least the participation) of lots of other people. All of these good things allow us to do something—define a type, either as a class or an interface; define and handle an exception (and tell others when to expect such an exception); or create a package that both defines a separate namespace and interacts with the protection mechanisms to give you a layer of abstraction.

Now we are going to turn to a good part of Java that lets us *not* do something. In the early days of Java, I used to ask people if they would be willing to try a programming tool that would fix over half of the bugs in their code. They were always eager to get such a tool; when I pointed out that it was Java, they were confused. The part of Java that allowed this claim (and still allows it) is garbage collection. Because of this feature, you don't have to do explicit memory management within your program, and flaws in such memory management have been shown to be a large fraction of the bugs in programs written in languages that don't have garbage collection.

Even though garbage collection is a feature that allows you to not do things, there are still some things that you have to understand to use the feature correctly. There are still ways to defeat the garbage collector and produce a memory leak. And habits from other languages, which conflate memory management with other forms of resource management and reclamation, don't translate well to Java. So we will talk about a feature that, at its best, should be transparent.

The Basics

The basics of garbage collection, at least from the programmer's view, are pretty simple.* Objects take up space in the memory of a computer. When we first create those objects, that memory is allocated. But memory is a finite resource. While memory is not nearly so finite these days as it used to be, we programmers have been very clever at using it up faster than the computer manufacturers can add it to systems. So when we are done with an object, we would like that memory to be reclaimed so it can be used for something else. In languages like C and C++, it was up to the programmer to explicitly free up such memory. Java is the first widely used system language† to include automatic garbage collection, where the runtime system keeps track of when an object will no longer be used and automatically frees up the memory space taken up by those objects.

You would think that cleaning up objects (and therefore freeing up memory) when a program is finished with the object would be a straightforward thing to do, and so automating that process shouldn't be that big a deal. If we were writing simple programs in which the lifetime of an object was easy to track, this might be the case. After all, this seems not that different from picking your socks up off the floor and putting them in the hamper, or recycling the soda cans that accumulate in your office (although programmers have the reputation for not being very good at either of these tasks).

The fact is that it is difficult to keep track of when and how to clean up the memory used by objects. There are the easy cases where an object is created at the beginning of a method, gets used inside of that method, and then is never used again when that method is finished. But most of the time when an object is created, it is handed to some other part of the program. That part of the program may store a reference to the object in some other object, which then gets handed to some other part of the program. Worse yet, a reference to the object might be stored in multiple objects, in which case it is up to the programmer working in a language that does not have garbage collection to keep track of when the last reference is gone so that the object can be cleaned up. Programmers have to make it clear in routines that create objects which one is responsible for deleting those objects and under what circumstances. Get rid of an object too soon, and those who think they have a reference to a still-existing object will (if they are lucky) have a reference to nothing, or (if they are unlucky) have a reference to a new object, which may have nothing in common with the old object.

---

* It must be stressed that this simplicity is only for the user of garbage collection. If you are trying to implement garbage collection, things are devilishly hard, which is one of the reasons that garbage collection took so long to become part of widely used languages.

† Before my mailbox is filled with angry email from former Lisp or Smalltalk programmers, let me hasten to add that Java was not the first language to have garbage collection, or even the first system language that had garbage collection. Like most of the other features of Java, garbage collection was well known in other languages first; that is one of the reasons that it was added to Java.

Studies done around the time of the introduction of the Java language claimed that over half of the bugs in C and C++ programs were caused by problems with memory management.[‡] Not only are such bugs common, but they also are notoriously difficult to track down. An effect of a memory leak or the use of memory that has already been freed often cannot be seen until well after the code that caused the problem was run, and would often go away when the problematic program was run in the debugger (because the debugger would move the program to a different location in memory). Tools have been invented that track the use of memory, and will tell a programmer when some piece of memory is reused too early or not freed at all. While these tools identify the problems, they don't help a programmer solve the problem. Knowing that you aren't freeing up some memory is a first step in finding the problem, but the real problem is determining where and when you can discard the memory used. Garbage collection does all of this for the programmer, simplifying the writing of programs and libraries and making the programs themselves more robust.

Garbage Collection and References

Even though garbage collection is invisible to the programmer, there are lots of effects of garbage collection that leave their marks all over the language. The most obvious of these are the lack of pointers in Java and the use of references everywhere.

In languages such as C or C++, there are objects (or structures) and there are pointers to those objects. The C notion of a pointer is really an address in memory; the value of a pointer is a real place (or as real as virtual memory allows it to be) that is the location in the store where your data is located. If you have an object `foo` with a field `bar`, you get the value of the field by `foo.bar`. But if `fooptr` is a pointer to `foo`, you get the value held in field `bar` with `foo->bar`. It's like dealing with the White Knight in *Through the Looking Glass*—you need to be careful about whether you are talking about the thing or what the thing is called.

In the Java language, there is only a single way to access an object, and it is a reference. A reference is like a pointer in C or C++, in that it is an indirect mechanism allowing access to objects in memory. But it is unlike a pointer in every other way. You can't access the reference itself, and in particular you can't get a reference to a reference in the way you can get a pointer to a pointer. You can't do arithmetic with a reference; adding 1 to a pointer in C gives you another pointer, but adding 1 to a Java reference either adds one to the object referenced or gives you a compilation error. All you can do with a reference (other than passing it around to others) is to access fields or methods of the object to which the reference refers.

[‡] See, for example, George Belotsky, "C++ Memory Management: From Fear to Triumph" (*http://linuxdevcenter.com/pub/a/linux/2003/05/08/cpp_mm-1.html*), or Venu Dasigi, "A Catalog of Common Bugs in C++ Programming" (*http://cs.spsu.edu/vdasigi/Debugging/CCSC99pap.pdf*).

Much has been made of the security aspects of Java references. By having references rather than pointers and not allowing arithmetic on references, the Java environment avoids a lot of the bugs and security vulnerabilities that are caused by allowing such manipulation in C or C++. But this is a bonus outcome, a happy byproduct of Java having references. The real reason references are part of Java is because of garbage collection.

Garbage collection requires that the system know the difference between references to objects and other forms of data. This allows the system to keep track of what objects are referenced, and remove objects when there are no longer any references to them. Pointers look just like integers, and so it is difficult for the system to tell the difference between a real pointer and something that might be a pointer but is, in fact, simply a value.

An environment that includes garbage collection also needs to be able to move memory objects when needed. Otherwise, the memory that is being used can become fragmented (as garbage is collected), and there are lots of optimizations that require that objects be moved. For example, generational garbage collectors depend on the observation that most objects are short-lived. They are allocated, used briefly, and then never used again. This means that if an object is used for some extended period of time, it is much less likely to become garbage in the near future. So generational collectors keep two heaps of objects. One of those heaps contains new objects, which are likely to be collected the next time the garbage collector is run. The other heap contains objects that have existed for some period of time (often those that have survived a first garbage-collection sweep). When an object is determined to be long-lived, it is moved from the new-object heap to the old-object heap. This older heap does not need to be collected nearly as regularly as the new heap, meaning that less time needs to be spent on garbage collection in general.

But if objects are going to be moved around, you need to make sure that those objects can still be found and used by anyone who wants to access the object. This requires that the objects be referenced only indirectly, and that the program cannot look into the reference (since the program might see information that, after a garbage collection and a move, would be invalid). It also means that if we were able to add or subtract some value to a reference and get another reference, there is no assurance that the next time we did that same operation we would get a reference to the same object (or to anything, for that matter).

For both of these reasons (and probably others), Java has references rather than pointers. This is a good thing, freeing up the programmer from thinking about memory management and allowing the system to globally manage the memory in a program. Because of garbage collection, it is not only easier to write programs in Java, but it is more likely that your program is not subject to memory leaks and is more secure. All good things to get, especially if it doesn't require you to think about it.

Memory Leaks

Because the Java platform has garbage collection, you might think that there is no way that you can get into the kinds of memory management problems that are the bane of the C or C++ programmer's existence. In some cases, this is true; you won't find yourself using the same piece of memory for two different objects in Java, or writing to a memory location that hasn't been allocated (although you can get into trouble trying to dereference a `null` pointer). But programmers are very clever people, so there are still ways to leak memory, even if the computer is cleaning up after you.

Memory leaks occur in Java programs not because you as the programmer forget to deallocate some memory, but because you as a programmer forget and leave a reference to an object hanging around in some other object when that reference is no longer needed. The way garbage collection works is to find each object for which there is no longer a live reference in the program. But a live reference is simply any reference in any other live object (or object thought to be live) in the program. So forgetting to get rid of a reference can mean that an object hangs around far longer than you ever intended. For many objects, this is not a problem. Most objects are small, and most programs don't run for that long. But for large objects, or long-running programs, such memory leaks can pile up. The result is the same kind of waxy-yellow object buildup that you can get without garbage collection, along with lower performance and huge heaps.

Suppose, for example, that we want to keep track not only of the statistics for individual baseball players, but also for teams. To do this, we will need to aggregate a group of players into a team. We will start by introducing a base interface of a `Player` that will contain the various roles that we have already defined. Players will have names, but we will also assign identifiers to them (since different players might have the same name, and we don't want to be confused). Each player will also have a position and be part of a team. Such an interface might look something like:

```
package org.oreilly.javaGoodParts.examples.statistics;

import java.util.UUID;

/**
 *Basic interface for a player object.
 *
 */
public interface Player {

    enum Position {
        Pitcher, Catcher, FirstBase, SecondBase,
        ThirdBase, ShortStop, LeftField, CenterField,
        RightField, DH, Utility
    }
```

```
/**
 * Return the identifier for the player. This is just
 * an <code>int</code>, generated when the player object is
 * first created, used to distinguish between players
 * that might have the same name.
 */
UUID getId();

/**
 * Return the name of the player, as a <code>String</code>
 */
String getName();

/**
 * Return a <code>String</code> that is the name of the
 * team for this player.
 */
Team getTeam();

/**
 * Return the <code>Position</code> played by this player
 * @return the <code>Position</code> of this player,
 * which will be used to determine the roles that the
 * player has.
 */
Position getPosition();

/**
 * Set the <code>Position</code> of the player
 * @param pos the <code>Position</code> played
 * by this player.
 */
void setPosition(Position pos);
}
```

We can now collect a group of players into a Team, a container type that might have an interface something like:

```
package org.oreilly.javaGoodParts.examples.statistics;

import java.util.List;
/**
 * The <code>Team</code> interface, which defines
 * the notion of a team for our statistics package. A
 * team is, at first incarnation, simply a collection of
 * players. All teams have a name.
 */
public interface Team {
    /**
     * Return a <code>String</code> that is the name of
     * this team.
     */
    String getName();
    /**
     * Return a list of the players that are on this
     * team.
```

```
    */
    List<? extends Player> getPlayerList();
    /**
     * Add a player to the team.
     */
    void addPlayer(Player toAdd);
    /**
     * Remove a player from the team.
     */
    void removePlayer(Player toRemove);
}
```

This interface allows us to get the name of the team, assign a player to the team, remove a player from the team, and get a list of all of the players who are currently on the team. Note that we are using a parameterized list that allows us to get back not just a Player object but any object that extends the Player interface; we will talk more about parameterized types in Chapter 7.

The reason we are talking about these interfaces is that we now have an object (the Team object) that will contain references to Player objects. And because we now have a way to store references to an object, we also have a way to defeat the garbage collector. All we have to do to get a memory leak is to forget to remove a Player object from a Team when, say, a player retires (rather than being moved to a different team). We might not use that Player object anymore, but there will still be a reference to the object that can be traced and that will keep the garbage collector from reclaiming the space used by the object.

A memory leak in this case is not very likely, but anyone using Java needs to know that any compilation of references is a potential area for a memory leak. If there are numerous places where a reference to an object might be stored, we have to make sure that all of those references are deleted when we are done with the object. If any one of them remains, the object will remain, taking up the space that could otherwise be reused. So even though garbage collection frees us from having to think about when the memory taken up by an object can be reclaimed, we still need to be careful and make sure that when we are done with an object, we clear the references in our program to allow the garbage collector to do its work.

If it is still possible to have a memory leak, one might wonder if garbage collection really bought us anything in Java and if it should be considered a good part of the language. It doesn't take much thought to realize that the answer is still very much in the affirmative. Cases like the one just shown where we are leaking memory are caused by local errors. In our example, the local error was a failure to remove a reference from the collection when we were done with that reference. This is much easier to find than memory leaks in non-garbage-collected environments, where the problem is essentially global. Memory in such environments is leaked when there is no place in the program where it is clear that the object is no longer needed. This requires analyzing the entire program, a much more difficult job than tracking a localized bug.

Other Resources

Although garbage collection frees the programmer from having to manage memory, there are other resources that are used in a program that do require explicit management. File handles and sockets, for example, are also scarce resources (their scarcity will depend on the underlying operating system) that will be used in a program and need to be freed once they are no longer needed. Unlike memory, the Java environment does not help with the management of such resources.

There are programmers who try to delegate the management of such resources to the garbage collection system in Java. These attempts are usually done through the use of *finalizers*. In almost all cases, such attempts are misguided at best and just wrong at worst. It's worth taking a couple of minutes to talk about why.

A finalizer is a special method on a class that is run prior to any object of the class being garbage collected. Such methods look like:

```
protected void finalize() throws Throwable{
    ...
}
```

Finalizers are the duals of constructors. Just as a constructor is run when an object is created, a finalizer will be run when an object is about to be deleted by the garbage collector. You don't have to call a finalizer for it to run (indeed, explicitly calling a finalizer is almost certainly a mistake); that is taken care of by the garbage collection system.

There are lots of obviously bad things that you can do in a finalizer. One that almost everyone points out is using the finalizer to place a reference to the object being finalized (`this`) into some collection. Doing this resurrects the object, which means that the garbage collector will no longer free up the space used by the object (or delete the object). But as the genie in *Aladdin* said, bringing back the dead is a really bad idea. The genie was talking about people, but the same is true with objects.

A less obvious bad thing can be shown if we extend our `Player` example to include the ability to store `Player` objects in files. We do this by first making our `PlayerImpl` implement the `Serializable` interface (about which much more will be said in Chapter 9), add a private static field that is the `serialVersionUID` (also discussed in that later chapter), and add a set of fields to hold information that will be needed for reading from and writing to a file. Continuing the tradition of using the filesystem as a database, we will store the player records in files that are named using the `String` representation of the player's unique identifier, but we will also add a `String` field which will hold the prefix that will let us identify the location of the file (for example, the path to the directory that holds the file). We also add a field that will hold the `ObjectInputStream` that we will use to read the player information to the file.

Next, we add a constructor that allows us to create a **Player** object with data initialized from a file (if that file exists). This constructor takes a **String** (to identify the directory in which the player's file is located) and the player ID. If the file is found and read, the fields of the newly created **Player** object are initialized using the information from the file. If no file is found (or if there is another problem with the file), the **Player** object is created with an unknown name and the identifier passed in to the constructor.

Here is a first implementation of this scheme, complete with a finalizer (but eliding the code that we have already seen):

```
public class PlayerImpl implements Player, Serializable {

    private static final long serialVersionUID = 1;
    private UUID id;
    private String name;
    private String filePrefix;
    private Team team;
    private Position pos = Position.Utility;
    private boolean changed = false;

    public PlayerImpl(UUID playerId, String prefix) {
        id = playerId;
        filePrefix = prefix;
        try {
            ObjectInputStream readIn = new ObjectInputStream(
                    new FileInputStream(prefix + id.toString()));
            PlayerImpl copy = (PlayerImpl) readIn.readObject();
            readIn.close();
            id = playerId;
            name = copy.name;
            team = copy.team;
            pos = copy.pos;
        } catch (IOException e) {
            System.out.println(
                "unable to open file for player, creating new player object");
            name = "unknown";
        } catch (ClassNotFoundException e) {
            System.out.println("unable to read file for player");
        }
    }

    protected void finalize() {
        if (readIn != null) {
            try {
                readIn.close();
            } catch (Exception e) {
                /*if there is an exception on close, we will
                 * just eat it*/
                }
        }
        if (changed) {
            try {
                ObjectOutputStream writeOut = new ObjectOutputStream(
                        new FileOutputStream(filePrefix +
```

```
                        id.toString()));
                writeOut.writeObject(this);
                writeOut.close();
            } catch (Exception e) {
                System.out.println("unable to write object");
            }
        }
    }
```

In this version of the code, we leave the `ObjectInputStream` that we used to read in our `Player` state open. This allows us to reread the state at any time, without having to open the file again (an operation that can be quite expensive). Instead, we wait until the `Player` object is being garbage collected to close the `ObjectInputStream`, since we know that we won't be rereading the state then. At that time, we also check to see whether the `Player` object has been changed in any way (assuming that any object that mutates the state will change the altered field from false to true). If any change has occurred, we open up the file for writing and write the new state. We wait until the finalizer to do this to ensure that we don't waste any writes to the file before the program is finished with the object.

This approach has a nice symmetry; what gets done in the constructor gets undone in the finalizer, and in between, things should be fast and straightforward. But the approach contains two errors that will cause real problems. One of these errors is fairly obvious and will probably bite the program early (and often), and thus be relatively easy to deal with. The other is subtler, and causes the kinds of errors that are hard to understand because they seem to happen randomly.

The simpler of the two errors involves keeping the `ObjectInputStream` open from the creation of the `Player` object until that object is finalized. This ties the life cycle of the `ObjectInputStream` to the overall life cycle of the object, and merges the resource management of the stream with the memory management for the object. The problem with this is that an open `ObjectInputStream` takes up resources other than memory. In particular, an `ObjectInputStream` built from a `FileInputStream` keeps a file open, which takes up a file descriptor. These descriptors are themselves a finite resource. Depending on the operating system on which the virtual machine is running, you might have a lot of file descriptors, or you might have a much smaller number. On a modern computer, the number of file descriptors is certainly much smaller than the amount of memory available. So tying the management of file descriptors to the management of memory is connecting the management of a scarce resource with the management of a much less scarce resource. More importantly, the number of available file descriptors is almost certainly smaller than the number of players for whom we are keeping statistics. As the number of `Player` objects increases, you will run out of file descriptors, and the program written in the style shown earlier will fail.

Fixing this problem is straightforward. We simply need to move the code that closes the `ObjectInputStream` out of the finalizer and put it back in the constructor. Rather than leaving the `ObjectInputStream` open during the time that the `Player` object exists,

---

we will leave it open only when we are actively reading the contents of the stream. If we need to reread the object, we will open the stream again. Although this might take some time, it is much less error-prone than keeping the stream open during the entire program. By closing the `ObjectInputStream` when we are finished using it, we explicitly manage the resource of the file descriptors, freeing them up as soon as we no longer need them. We can also simplify our private data structure that we use to keep track of the state of the `Player`. We no longer need to keep the `ObjectInputStream` reference in the `Player` object; instead, we will keep the pathname that, with the player identifier, can be used to find that file again. So we win all around.

The second, and subtler, bug is the result of our deciding to write any updated state for the `Player` object during finalization. This seems like a good idea. After all, we can be guaranteed that nothing else is going to change after the finalization call, so this is the time when we can really check to see whether anything needs to be saved and, if it does, do the writing.

The problem with this approach is that there is no guarantee that the finalizer will ever be called on an object. Finalizers are run in an asynchronous fashion, which means that you can't tell exactly when they will be run. The only guarantee is that the finalizer will run after there are no active references to an object, but before that object is fully garbage collected. This means that it is possible for the program to end (and the Java Virtual Machine to exit) without invoking the finalizer for all of the objects that were created in the program. Your virtual machine might guarantee that all finalizers are called, but some other virtual machine might not. And if the finalizer does not get called, then the code we have used to update our `Player` state may not get called, and we can lose some updates.

This kind of bug can drive you crazy. You can go for a long time and never have the bug appear. As long as the finalizer gets called, things work just fine. But as soon as the finalizer doesn't get called, updates are lost. And you have to figure out why something that was working isn't anymore.

There are a couple of things that we could do to avoid this problem. One is to update the player state when it gets changed, knowing that we might have to update it multiple times during a program run, but at least being sure that we won't lose any updates. The other would be to have a shutdown method on the whole program that goes through all of the `Player` objects that have been created during a program run and explicitly calls a method that does the work now done in the finalizer. We could even call the finalizer explicitly. As we said before, calling a finalizer is generally a sign that something is wrong, but you can make the call. Finalizers, after all, are just methods like any other, and can be called by any other part of the program. Of course, if you are doing anything else in a finalizer that you don't want to happen more than once, then explicitly calling the finalizer would not be a good idea. Generally, it is better to do your work in other, less magic methods.

My own experience is that use of a finalizer is generally a sign that something is wrong in my program. The magic tie between these methods and the garbage collection system introduces an asynchronous uncertainty that makes these methods much less useful than they might, on first examination, appear to be. The fact that you don't know when or even if such methods will be called makes them at best the place to put some last-chance-checking code in objects that hold references to some kind of resource. Even then, the most a finalizer should do is make sure that the resource has been freed up by other code, and clean up if it has not.

Given all of this, we change our `PlayerImpl` class to look like:

```java
package org.oreilly.javaGoodParts.examples.impl;

import java.io.FileInputStream;
import java.io.FileOutputStream;
import java.io.IOException;
import java.io.ObjectInputStream;
import java.io.ObjectOutputStream;
import java.io.Serializable;
import java.util.UUID;
import org.orielly.javaGoodParts.examples.statistics.Player;
import org.orielly.javaGoodParts.examples.statistics.Team;

/**
 *
 */
public class PlayerImpl implements Player, Serializable {

    private static final long serialVersionUID = 1;
    private UUID id;
    private String name;
    private String filePrefix;
    private Team team;
    private Position pos = Position.Utility;
    private boolean changed = false;

    public PlayerImpl(String playerName) {
        name = playerName;
        id = UUID.randomUUID();
    }

    public PlayerImpl(UUID playerId, String prefix) {
        id = playerId;
        filePrefix = prefix;
        try {
            ObjectInputStream readIn = new ObjectInputStream(
                    new FileInputStream(prefix + id.toString()));
            PlayerImpl copy = (PlayerImpl) readIn.readObject();
            readIn.close();
            id = playerId;
            name = copy.name;
            team = copy.team;
            pos = copy.pos;
        } catch (IOException e) {
```

```
                System.out.println(
                        "unable to open file for player, creating new player object");
                name = "unknown";
            } catch (ClassNotFoundException e) {
                System.out.println("unable to read file for player");
            }
        }

    protected void writeState() {
        try {
            ObjectOutputStream writeOut =
                    new ObjectOutputStream(new FileOutputStream(
                    filePrefix + id.toString()));
            writeOut.writeObject(this);
            writeOut.close();
            changed = false;
        } catch (Exception e) {
            System.out.println("unable to write object");
            e.printStackTrace();
        }
    }

    protected void finalize(){
        if (changed){
            writeState();
            System.out.println("writing state in finalizer");
        }
    }
    ...
}
```

Our constructor that reads in a `Player` state from the filesystem now closes the `ObjectInputStream` immediately after the read. We now have a `writeState()` method that will write any changed state to the filesystem and update the changed flag to show that the state in the filesystem is the same as the state in the program. We still have a finalizer, but all it does is a last-gasp check on the changed flag. If, somehow, a mistake has been made in the program and some alteration of the `Player` state has been made without a call to `writeState()`, the finalizer will make the call to update the permanent record. This is the coding equivalent of wearing both a belt and suspenders, and is evidence of a level of paranoia that is common among software developers. If such a call is made, we will also display a message, since writing state in the finalizer shows that some change isn't being recorded in the main body of the program. This is a lurking bug that we will want to fix.

Also note that the exception handling in the `writeState()` method is completely inadequate. If this were anything other than an example in a book, I would have to do something very different to make sure that the new state is actually saved. But since it is just an example in a book, I will merely apologize.

The moral of this story is, at bottom, that we should not be greedy. Garbage collection is one of the good things about Java, and it is a good thing that makes our programs more reliable without requiring us to do all the hard thinking about memory manage-ment that we had to do with earlier languages. But we shouldn't mistake the help Java gives us in the area of memory management as a license to forget about all of the scarce resources that our program might be using. Although we can tie the management of such resources to the garbage collector, doing so is probably a bad idea. Instead, we can use those ties as a final check. But we shouldn't use it for more than that, or depend on the garbage collector to do our work for us.

CHAPTER 6

The Java Virtual Machine

We all know that the best things in life are free. In a similar way, the best things in a language or computing environment are the things that we don't have to think about at all. These are the things that are intellectually free. By not having to think about them, we free ourselves to think about other things. The task of programming—especially the task of programming large, long-lived systems of programs—is hard enough that anything we can use and not think about is a good thing.

In Java, it is the virtual machine that gives us a huge amount of functionality without requiring that we give back much, if any, thought. Most of the time, the virtual machine is to the Java programmer what water is to a fish. It is the environment in which we live, through which we move, and from which we draw our basic sustenance. But we rarely think about it, and when we do, it is generally because something about it has gotten in our way, is doing something unexpected, or we have to figure out how to configure the thing to run faster or better.

Since we as Java programmers think about the virtual machine only when it needs care and feeding (or when it is getting in our way), we often forget what it is doing for us. But the virtual machine changes the way we have to think about building large systems and has made that job much easier. So it is fitting that we spend a few pages to step back and think a bit about the Java virtual machine (hereafter simply the JVM), as understanding what the JVM does for us is central to understanding much of the power of Java.

The Basics

Virtual machines, and the notion of virtualization in general, are all the rage these days. Whole companies have been built around particular virtual machines, and there is an array of choices from vendors and from the open source world for those who want to explore the world of virtual machines.

Most of the virtual machines* that people are paying attention to virtualize at a very low level. These virtual machines provide a software layer between the raw hardware and the operating system, giving the OS a set of calls that allow that system to boot and interact with the hardware using a single software interface. Using such virtual machines, a single computer can run multiple operating systems at the same time, since the operating system now runs on a virtual rather than physical machine. These virtual machines are really virtual hardware environments. We programmers interact with these virtual machines in the same way that we interact with all pure hardware environments. Which is to say, not at all, except through the mediation of an operating system, which really provides us with a set of abstractions that we can use directly.

The Java virtual machine is a similar sort of abstraction, but done at a much higher level. Rather than presenting a single set of interfaces and abstractions representing hardware to an operating system, the JVM presents an abstraction of both the hardware and the operating system to the programmer. This means that the virtual machine presents more than an abstract view of some piece of hardware. All of the functions of the computer, from the filesystem to networking to threads, are presented as part of the programming environment. This makes the JVM and its associated environment much more complex than the virtual machines that are mimicking hardware, but also means that the programmer deals directly with one set of abstractions on all of the implementations of the virtual machine. A JVM on one operating system should look to the programmer just like a JVM on a completely different operating system. If it doesn't, it isn't because your code isn't using the operating system correctly; it is because of a flaw in the JVM. It's someone else's problem.

The difference in the abstraction level presented by the JVM and that presented by the low-level VMs is in part a function of the intended use for those virtual machines. The Java virtual machine was always meant to be a development and runtime platform for new code, written in the Java language. Virtual machines such as Xen or VMWare are meant to be platforms that allow system administrators to run existing code, written to existing operating systems, in a way that lets the system administrator leverage the hardware in a machine room in an efficient manner. Running those existing applications requires running the operating system on which those existing applications were originally targeted, so a low-level abstraction below those operating systems makes sense. But for the production of new code, the JVM makes sense, since it papers over the differences between the various operating systems.

The mechanism for this splits the work of generating object code between the compiler and the JVM. The Java compiler translates the source code into a file of bytecodes, which are then run within the JVM. Each source file will generate at least a single bytecode file.† The JVM is then responsible for loading that file, and the files that it

---

* Examples of the sorts of virtual machines I'm talking about here are VMWare's products (both server and desktop), Xen, VirtualBox, and the like. This is hardly an exhaustive list; more seem to appear weekly.

† Note that files that have inner classes, which I do not discuss in this book, will generate multiple bytecode files.

references, into the virtual machine, which will then interpret and run the bytecodes. Early JVMs acted as an interpreter for the bytecodes, translating those codes into whatever underlying instructions were required by the basic hardware and operating system.

This is not a particularly novel approach to computing. The UCSD Pascal system did essentially the same thing in 1978. The compiler for the Pascal language in that system generated p-code (the equivalent of Java bytecodes) that was then run in a virtual machine, hiding the differences in the underlying hardware and operating system from the users of the system. The major difference between the UCSD system and the JVM is that the UCSD system ran on early personal computers or PDP-11s, whereas the JVM runs on much more modern equipment. This difference in speed of the underlying hardware was the difference between the painfully slow UCSD system and a more than adequate implementation of the JVM.

When Java was first introduced, all JVMs ran the bytecodes through an interpreter. But within a couple of years, the first just-in-time compilers were introduced. These compilers, which first appeared in research languages such as Self, would take the bytecodes that were being interpreted and compile them, on the fly, into native code. The most interesting thing about these compilers is that the more some piece of code was used, the more optimized the compiled code would be. Just-in-time compilation also has the advantage of knowing the actual usage of the code and the environment of the current program execution, so rather than having to optimize for all possible runs (like a standard, single-time compiler and optimizer), the just-in-time compiler can optimize for each particular run of the program. In theory, this should enable programs that are compiled on the fly to be faster than those that are compiled in more traditional fashion; in fact, such results are beginning to be seen with the current crop of virtual machines.

The JVM has been a remarkably stable abstraction, even though the implementation of the JVM has undergone considerable change over the years. Bytecodes that are generated by earlier versions of the Java compiler still run on the modern implementations of the JVM, although they do so much more quickly than on the earlier JVM. There have been some changes to the basic JVM in the past couple of years, but these changes have been additions that allow other languages to compile to Java bytecodes and run within the JVM. Indeed, there are a number of other languages that now make use of the JVM as their operating environment, including Python (in the Jython incarnation) and functional languages such as Scala. There are versions of FORTH, LOGO, and Pascal that run on the JVM. There is Ruby, JavaScript, PHP, and no doubt others that I've not heard about. I have heard that are even tools that will convert COBOL programs into Java so that the programs can be run on the JVM (I have not verified this, nor do I intend to).

The point to this is that the JVM has become more than just a virtual machine for Java. It is now a runtime environment for lots of different languages, offering enough value on its own that it no longer needs to be tied to the particular syntax and semantics of the Java language. Even though it was not originally intended to be a virtual machine for more than Java, it has become close to the default platform for new object code.

That in itself makes the JVM interesting. But there are reasons for the JVM being the runtime environment of choice for such new code, and understanding what those are will help us gain a better understanding of the good parts of the JVM.

Security

One of the great things that the JVM provides is enhanced security, both for the programs running in the virtual machine and for the machine on which the JVM is executing. Since a Java program runs inside a JVM, there is an extra layer between the program and the computer. This extra layer has a lot of checks on the code, and isolates the code further from other code running on the physical machine. This lets the JVM act as a security monitor, and a lot of what the JVM does is tied to this role.

One of the ways that the JVM provides security is that it verifies all the code run in the JVM prior to loading that code. As part of loading a Java class into a running program, the JVM goes through a set of checks on the code. The highest level explanation is that the verifier makes sure that the bytecodes could have been produced by a conformant Java language compiler. In detail, this means that no types have been coerced in an incorrect way, there are no jumps to random parts of the code, and all the sequences of bytecodes make sense.

There has been considerable research and controversy over whether or not the verification performed by the JVM before classes are loaded is really sufficient to give complete security. Most of the common mechanisms that can be used to build malware (such as overwriting arrays or doing coercions on types) are not allowed in code loaded into the JVM, but there are occasional claims that new exploits have been found that may leak information or otherwise provide a handle for bad actors.

That there might be such exploits becomes much less surprising when one understands the origin of the verifier in the JVM. The original intention of the verifier was not to protect against attacks in code, but rather to make sure that there were fewer bugs in code. The Java language and environment was first invented to provide a programming environment for embedded devices. Such devices are widely deployed (when successful) and hard to patch, and the owners of such devices expect the devices to work (unlike users of software, who have learned better). Most of the features that were originally seen as part of the Java security model (garbage collection, references rather than pointers, bounds checking on arrays) were not introduced into the language to avoid malicious code, but to avoid buggy code. It was then realized that the difference between an attack and a bug was often the intention of the programmer, so these features were also seen as security enhancements.

The JVM also has a set of security models that can enforce different access rights on different parts of code. I'm not going to talk about this security model (or, perhaps more accurately, the set of security models that have been layered on top of each other) since it is complex, difficult to understand, and generally ignored or overwritten by users (who almost all have security policy files that allow all code to have all permissions). This is a book about the good parts of Java, and I'm not convinced that the security mechanisms should be included. This is not to say that those who invented the series of Java security models and mechanisms weren't very smart people with the best of intentions. But like many other security systems, both inside and outside of the Java environment, getting good security often requires trading off usability.

But the flaws in verification and complexity of the security model should not obscure an important fact about the JVM with respect to security. Java in general, and the JVM in particular, try to give the programmer a secure environment. It may not be fully immune from the most sophisticated attacks, but it is better than most other alternatives. It is somewhat ironic that the JVM has been so often faulted for security failures when it is one of the few environments that has attempted to give some measure of security. Go figure. Even with its flawed security, Java as an environment is more secure than the alternatives.

Because the JVM enforces a security model that was originally tied to the Java language, it is not always possible to have a language hosted on the JVM that is exactly like the language when it is compiled to native object code. The bytecodes generated for every language will be the Java bytecodes, and the restrictions enforced by the verifier on sequences of bytecodes are tied to the Java language. So if you are using a language that generates bytecodes so that you can use the JVM as your virtual machine, make sure to check the small print of the documentation. There may be some language idioms that are outlawed in the hybrid environment, but many of those that are outlawed are restricted for your own good. Not having them makes for a more secure program.

Portability

The security offered by the JVM is a good thing, and it certainly gets a lot of press and a lot of discussion. But the real reason that the JVM is a good thing is that it makes the code you write portable. That is, the JVM isolates you from the chip and the operating system on which your program is going to run in such a way that any program that you write ought to run on any computer and operating system that has a JVM. And I'm not talking about your source code; I'm talking about the object code. Take a Java binary, move it from machine to machine and operating system to operating system, and the program will run.

This has always been the point of Java's "write once, run anywhere" slogan. This is also why the higher-level virtual machine that the JVM offers is so important, and why the JVM is different from the kinds of virtual machines that simply virtualize the hardware. The JVM does not just offer a layer of abstraction on top of the chip. The JVM offers a layer of abstraction on the chip, the disk, the network, any other hardware, and the operating system itself. It is, of course, more than just the raw JVM itself. It is a combination of the JVM and the libraries that are included with that virtual machine that give this portability. But the combination of the virtual machine and the libraries that go with it give a kind of portability that is unmatched.

Maybe programmers who have grown up in the age of the JVM (that is, the last dozen or so years) don't realize what a revolution this is in the way programming is done. It used to be[‡] that writing portable code meant adding a lot of `#defines` and `ifdefs` to your code, and having makefiles that would determine the environment and generate the actual makefile that would define enough context for your code that you could get the code compiled. And when that was done, you could start debugging, since the semantics of a library call on one OS might be quite different from the semantics of that same call on another OS.[§] And you needed to do this for every combination of processor and operating system on which you wanted your code to run.

Things have gotten somewhat simpler over time just because of the consolidation of the computer industry. There used to be a lot more variation in processors and a lot more different operating systems than there are today. But even if you confine yourself to the major chip architecture and the major operating systems, you probably have at least four combinations that you have to worry about (Windows, Mac, and the two Linux flavors-of-the-day). And the mobile phone manufacturers are making me feel young again, insisting that each phone have its own processor and operating environment that are incompatible with any other phone's processor and operating environment.

With the JVM, things are different. If there is a JVM on the environment, your program will run. The same way it does with every other JVM. Or it is someone else's problem. Which means that instead of tearing your hair out trying to fix your code, you can file a bug with the Java organization and get the problem fixed.

I remember the first time that I realized the power of the JVM with respect to portability. This was long ago (Java 1.0 had just been released), and my lab group had built a couple of large libraries (Remote Method Invocation and Object Serialization, to be precise) and a couple of demos of the then-new technology. All our work had been on Sun Sparc systems running Solaris. But we wanted to show that the new libraries were cross-platform, so we wanted to run a client on Windows and the server on Unix.

We had copied our complete source tree over to a Windows box and were about to issue the `make` command when we stopped. Java was supposed to be portable. So, just for yucks, we simply copied the object files to the Windows box and fired up the demo. It just worked. After we got our jaws off the floor, we finally understood what this virtualization thing was all about.

---

‡ OK, I know that when you see a sentence starting with "it used to be," you immediately brace yourself for tales of how bad it was in the olden days. And yes, I did have to walk to school through the snow. But this is different, and important, so read on.

§ Actually, when the semantics of the library call was quite different, you were glad because that was the easy case. It was when the semantics were different only in subtle ways, generally in corner cases, that true madness could occur.

The overall Java environment has taken a lot of grief over the "write once, run any-where" slogan. Sometimes this grief is justified. The graphics may not be exactly the same on all systems. And it is true that although your code may run on all the JVMs‖ that are around, they may not run optimally, leading to the notion of "write once, *tune* everywhere." Those doing numerically intensive scientific programming certainly object to the inability of Java to take advantage of specialized floating-point features in various platforms (and are more than willing to give up getting the same answer on all platforms if that is the price of the added efficiency). And there are times when it isn't even clear what it means to "run everywhere." I remember long discussions in the earlier days of Java on whether "running everywhere" meant that your program would look the same everywhere, or meant that your program would adopt the "look and feel" of the platform on which it was running without changing the code. Each of these was a plausible interpretation (at least, each was supported by some member of the Java community), but they were mutually incompatible.

Although many of these criticisms may be true, the fact is that the JVM gives the programmer a better virtualization platform than any other. Writing portable Java code is not only possible, it is the default. Writing portable code in any other system language is very difficult. And for system programming (which often confines its graphical user interface to `println()` and `read()`), the problems with portability are rarely encountered.

Portability Traps

But saying that such problems are rarely encountered doesn't mean that they are never encountered (otherwise, I would have said "never"). Avoiding these problems generally requires that you be aware of operating system or other platform idiosyncrasies, and then find the proper abstraction within the Java system that will let you avoid these idiosyncrasies.

As an example of this, let's revisit some of the code that we wrote in Chapter 5 that allowed us to read and write the player data to the filesystem. As you may recall, we wrote the player information into a file that was named using the player's unique identifier. But that file was placed in the filesystem based on a `String` set during construction that we called the `filePrefix`. The intuition was that we would use the `filePrefix` field to identify the directory that would contain the file named with the player's unique ID. To refresh your memory, here is the code as we left it before:

```
package org.oreilly.javaGoodParts.examples.impl;

import java.io.FileInputStream;
import java.io.FileOutputStream;
```

‖ I am, of course, talking about all of the JVMs that are of the Java Standard Edition or above. The JVMs for J2ME, which are designed to run on phones, are not always subject to the uniformity being discussed in this chapter.

```java
import java.io.IOException;
import java.io.ObjectInputStream;
import java.io.ObjectOutputStream;
import java.io.Serializable;
import java.util.UUID;
import org.oreilly.javaGoodParts.examples.statistics.Player;
import org.oreilly.javaGoodParts.examples.statistics.Team;

/**
 *
 */
public class PlayerImpl implements Player, Serializable {

    private static final long serialVersionUID = 1;
    private UUID id;
    private String name;
    private String filePrefix;
    private Team team;
    private Position pos = Position.Utility;
    private boolean changed = false;

    public PlayerImpl(String playerName) {
        name = playerName;
        id = UUID.randomUUID();
    }

    public PlayerImpl(UUID playerId, String prefix) {
        id = playerId;
        filePrefix = prefix;
        try {
            ObjectInputStream readIn = new ObjectInputStream(
                    new FileInputStream(prefix + id.toString()));
            PlayerImpl copy = (PlayerImpl) readIn.readObject();
            readIn.close();
            id = playerId;
            name = copy.name;
            team = copy.team;
            pos = copy.pos;
        } catch (IOException e) {
            System.out.println(
                    "unable to open file for player, creating new player object");
            name = "unknown";
        } catch (ClassNotFoundException e) {
            System.out.println("unable to read file for player");
        }
    }

    protected void writeState() {
        try {
            Integer playerId = id;
            ObjectOutputStream writeOut =
                    new ObjectOutputStream(new FileOutputStream(filePrefix +
                            playerId.toString()));
            writeOut.writeObject(this);
            writeOut.close();
```

```
            changed = false;
        } catch (Exception e) {
            System.out.println("unable to write object");
            e.printStacktrace();
        }
    }

    protected void finalize(){
        if (changed){
            writeState();
            System.out.println(
                "writing state in finalizer");
        }
        ...
    }
```

The problem with this is that most filesystems are hierarchical, so you have a set of directory names that traverse the hierarchy to the point where files are stored. Part of this hierarchy is a separator character, which is used to separate the name of one directory from that of another. And these separator characters can (and do) differ from operating system to operating system. Since the `filePrefix` string will almost certainly contain a number of occurrences of the file separator character, how do we ensure that it will be the right character for the operating system on which the program is running?

Like a good library writer, we have actually finessed this problem in the code we have written. The way things are now set up, all of the separator characters have to be in the prefix argument that is passed in to the `PlayerImpl` constructor. But this means that any code calling the constructor will have to be very careful, not only to make sure that they end the `prefix` `String` with a filesystem separator but also to make sure that they don't hardcode in the kind of separator used in their development system in the prefix, thus making their code nonportable.

We can do a lot better than that. And in doing so, we can take a look at some of the mechanisms that the JVM offers to help us ensure that our code is actually portable, even in the face of various changes in operating systems and environments. Our strategy will be to take some of the pressure off the caller of our `Player` class. Rather than putting the onus on the caller to supply a place in the filesystem for us to store the data for a player, we will do much of the work ourselves. We will store the players in a directory that is determined by the team that the player is on. The team directories, in turn, will be stored in a directory that is determined when the program is run rather than by some code that we will write. This means that we are going to have to do something about the file separator character, since we will be building strings that include that character, and we will need to do that in a way that is portable. Fortunately, the JVM and the associated runtime environment give us ways to do this.

Actually, the JVM gives us a couple of ways to do this, which is more a statement about the history and evolution of the platform than an example of good software design. In a perfect (or even better) world, there would be one way to make our code portable with respect to things like the separator used in the filesystem. But in the world we are in, there are at least two.

We should start by thinking about what the filesystem organization should be for our Player data. Since we are naming the files using the unique identifiers that we are associating with the Player objects, we could just keep all of the files containing the data in a single directory, knowing that they will all have a unique name. But that would lead to a messy directory, so we would like to impose some grouping of the objects. Since we are talking about baseball players, the obvious grouping is by the team the player is on, which is information that we are already tracking in the Player object. So we will create a directory for each team and store the data for the players on that team in files within that directory. We can't assume that the names of the players are unique, but we can assume that the names of the teams are unique, so there is no need to add a unique identifier to the Team object.

Using this approach, constructing the filename is easy enough. We just have to concatenate the String that is the team name with the String that can be generated from the player ID. Between the two, we need to have the file path separator. This last is the operating-system-dependent part of the string, and if we just hardcode a \ or a / into our method (depending on which flavor of operating system we are using for development), our code won't be portable when moved to a system of a different flavor.

Fortunately, the Java environment gives us a way to deal with this. As part of the File class, there are static members that allow us to get the filename separator that is used by the system on which the code is running. We can get the separator either as a character or as a String. Since we are going to be concatenating this with a couple of other String objects, we will get the separator as a String. So our first cut at a revised PlayerImpl will have filenaming in the constructor and the writeState() method that looks like:

```
public PlayerImpl(UUID playerId, String teamName) {
    try {
        id = playerId;
        ObjectInputStream readIn =
                new ObjectInputStream(new FileInputStream(
                teamName + File.separator + id.toString())));
        PlayerImpl fromDisk = (PlayerImpl) readIn.readObject();
        readIn.close();
        id = playerId;
        name = fromDisk.name;
        team = fromDisk.team;
        pos = fromDisk.pos;
    } catch (IOException e) {
        System.out.println("unable to open file for player,
        creating new player   object");
        name = "unknown";
    } catch (ClassNotFoundException e) {
        System.out.println("unable to read file for player");
    }
}
```

```
    protected void writeState() {
        try {
            ObjectOutputStream writeOut =
                    new ObjectOutputStream(new FileOutputStream(
                    team.getName() + File.separator + id.toString()));
            writeOut.writeObject(this);
            writeOut.close();
            changed = false;
        } catch (Exception e) {
            System.out.println("unable to write object");
        }
    }
}
```

In this code, we have replaced the `filePrefix` that was magically passed in by the code calling the `PlayerImpl` with code that constructs a real file path. By using the `File.separator`, we ensure that the file path we construct will work on any environment, no matter what separator is used in filenames in that environment. Using the facilities given us by the libraries and the runtime, we have made our code portable.

We used the `File.separator` static field because we were dealing with the filesystem, so looking in the `File` class for the `String` seems like an obvious choice. We could have easily thought that the abstraction might be something related to the system on which we were running our program, and therefore gone looking for some way of finding the right character in the `System` class. We would have succeeded; we can get the same information using properties associated with the system. There is a system property named `file.separator` that we could have used that would have given us the string needed in our code. If we were to use this method of obtaining the file separator, our creation of the `ObjectInputStream` would look like:

```
ObjectInputStream readIn =
        new ObjectInputStream(new FileInputStream(
        teamName + System.getProperty("file.separator")
        + Id.toString()));
```

and our call to write the player data would look like:

```
ObjectOutputStream writeOut =
        new ObjectOutputStream(new FileOutputStream(
        team.getName() + System.getProperty("file.separator")
        + playerId.toString()));
```

Although getting the separator character for our file path from the environment eliminates one source of nonportability, we still have gotten only halfway to a solution for our problem. We now have a way of placing the player data in a directory determined by the team of the player, but we are still reading from and writing to a relative path. That is, where we look for data and where we write our data will depend on where the program is run, since the file path that we are constructing is a relative path. This path will be relative to where the JVM is run, which generally can be hard to determine on modern systems, and almost certainly not where we would like to keep the data.

What we really want is some way to allow information about the particular environment on which the JVM is running to be passed into our program. And, in fact, we have such a mechanism in the properties that we saw in our last example.

The standard set of properties can be used to tell us about the particular Java virtual machine that we are using, and some of the file and path conventions of the underlying system. But we can introduce new properties as well. There are a number of ways to do this. We could have a properties file included in the meta-information directory of the *.jar* file that holds our application. But we simply want to have a property that will tell us where in the filesystem to place our set of team directories so we can store the Player information. For something this simple, we will just let whoever is using our application define a new system property on the command line (or in the script) that launches the program. The java command allows defining such a system property with the command-line option:

```
-D propertyName=value
```

Such a property will be added to the set of system properties that can be found in our program.

So all that is left is to define a name, and then write the code that uses that name. When defining the name, it is important to make sure that the name will be unique, so we will use the convention of building a dot-separated name that will begin with some identifier for our program, followed by the name of the particular property. Unlike the rather long names that are used with packages to make sure that they are unique, we can use a smaller name for a property. Properties need to be unique only within the scope of a single running JVM. Packages, since they scope the names of classes that may be reused almost anywhere, need to be globally unique, which requires more effort (and more characters). We will call our program Statistics and the property fileRoot. So on our command line we will need to add the option:

```
-DStatistics.fileRoot=...
```

where we replace the ... with the directory in our filesystem where we want to store the statistics. We should also come up with a reasonable default in case the user forgets (or decides against) supplying a directory. The system properties allow us to find out a couple of likely candidates, including the user's home directory or the current working directory for the user. We will use the first of these.

To add this to our code, we will start with a private method that we can use to find out where the user specified the files should go. This code looks like:

```java
private String getFileRoot(){
        String fileRoot = System.getProperty("Statistics.fileRoot");
        if (fileRoot == null){
            fileRoot = System.getProperty("user.dir");
        }
        fileRoot = fileRoot + System.getProperty("file.separator");
        return fileRoot;
    }
```

This code simply looks for the system property named `Statistics.fileRoot`. If there is no such property, the call will return null; in that case we use the property named by `user.dir`. We end up adding a file separator to the end, and return that to the caller as a string that is the directory in the filesystem where the directories for the various teams will be located.

Now all we need to do is add this prefix to the methods where we read or write the `PlayerImpl` data. This is just another string concatenation, so our constructor and `writeState()` methods now look like:

```
public PlayerImpl(int playerId, String teamName) {
    id = playerId;
    try {
        Integer Id = new Integer(playerId);
        ObjectInputStream readIn =
                new ObjectInputStream(new FileInputStream(
                getFileRoot() + teamName +
                System.getProperty("file.separator") + Id.toString())));
        PlayerImpl copy = (PlayerImpl) readIn.readObject();
        readIn.close();
        id = playerId;
        name = copy.name;
        team = copy.team;
        pos = copy.pos;
    } catch (IOException e) {
        System.out.println(
            "unable to open file for player, creating new player object");
        name = "unknown";
    } catch (ClassNotFoundException e) {
        System.out.println("unable to read file for player");
    }
}

protected void writeState() {
    try {
        Integer playerId = id;
        ObjectOutputStream writeOut =
                new ObjectOutputStream(new FileOutputStream(
                getFileRoot() + team.getName() +
                System.getProperty("file.separator") + playerId.toString())));
        writeOut.writeObject(this);
        writeOut.close();
        changed = false;
    } catch (Exception e) {
        System.out.println("unable to write object");
    }
}
```

Note that we still need to put the separator character between the team name and the player identifier string, but we do not need to do that between the result of `getFile Root()` and the team name, since the `getFileRoot()` added that for us.

The end result is code that will run on any operating system, since we are using the abstractions provided by the JVM (and the Java environment) to mask the differences in operating systems and filesystems. Although we had to take a little care with our code, we don't need separate configuration languages, build steps, or binaries for the various platforms on which we might like our code to run. Instead, the virtual machine that runs our Java program takes care of that for us. So we don't have to think about such things. Programming is hard enough as it is without adding new things to think about, so this aspect of the JVM is definitely a good part of Java.

CHAPTER 7

Javadoc

All programmers know that it is important to comment their code and write complete documentation for the system in which their code is a component. We know that the documentation is necessary to allow others to use our code. We know that comments are needed to explain what we are doing (or trying to do), so that when others read our code, they can understand it. We also realize that the "other" who needs these comments and documentation to help read our code could well be ourselves six months from now when a high-priority bug has been filed. Comments and documentation are very important.

All programmers also know that it is important to floss, to bathe regularly, to wear seatbelts and not talk on cellphones in the car, and to dress for success. And like all of these other things that we ought to do, when the pressure is on and deadlines loom, we tend to "forget" to do those things. After all, they don't directly lead to getting the code working. And they can be added later.

In times of stress, the first thing to go is the documentation. Comments are embedded in the code and so can be written along with it, but given enough deadline pressure we all find that the code is "self-documenting." Documentation, on the other hand, has traditionally been written outside of the code, often by another person (a tech writer), often after the code has been written, and often badly. Doing either later is never a good idea. In most cases, going back and adding comments or documentation never happens. Even when it does, the results are sketchy at best.

The Java platform doesn't solve this problem, but it makes the production of useful documentation much easier than it is in other environments. Java allows real documentation to be embedded with the code being documented, so that the two can be produced at the same time and, even more importantly, changed at the same time. The mechanism for this is Javadoc, which is definitely a good part of Java.

The Basics

When I first started programming, there was only one way to mark comments. When you wanted to have a comment in the code, you started a line with /* and then wrote your comment. When the comment was done, you ended the comment with */. The compiler ignored anything between the two. There was no nesting of comments (multiple instances of /* would be terminated by a single instance of */).*

Some time later, it was observed that there are really two kinds of comments that you want to put into your code. There are long comments, often spanning multiple lines, which are just fine for marking with the existing comment delimiters. But there are also times when a programmer just wants to make a short comment at the end of a line or on a single line, and the notion of having a comment delimiter that marked everything from the comment sign to the end of the line as a comment was born. C++ was the first language I used that had this kind of comment, where anything from a // until the end of the line was seen as a comment; standard C adopted this form of comment, as did Java. Soon, the type of comment that started with /* and ended with */ was known as a *block comment*, whereas those that started with // and ended with a line break were known as *line comments*.

Java added a third kind of comment, called *documentation comments*. These are like a block comment, but in addition to being ignored by the compiler, these comments are designed to be read by a separate tool, Javadoc. This tool then uses these comments to produce documentation for the code containing the comment. The tool that parses these comments was written when Java was seen as a programming environment for the Web, so the output of the tool is a set of *.html* files designed to be read as hypertext in a standard web browser.

Documentation comments begin with the characters /** and end with the characters */. This makes them a variant of block comments, and like block comments, multiple lines of text can appear between the delimiters. By convention, the beginning of every line in a documentation comment begins with the * character, but this is just convention. You can start the intervening lines with no special character and things will be just fine. But it isn't a bad convention, because it will remind you that those intervening lines are comments. Most IDEs (which is to say, both Eclipse and Netbeans) will automatically start a line in a documentation comment with a *.

Unlike standard comments, documentation comments can only appear in certain places in a source file. You may have a documentation comment prior to the declaration of a class or an interface or prior to the declaration of a method or a field in a class, but such comments will be ignored if they are placed in the body of a method. This is a reflection of the purpose of these comments. They are meant to document your interfaces, classes, and methods, but not the details of the implementations of those classes

---

* Actually, when I first started programming, a comment was indicated by having a "C" character in column 1 of the card, just before the sequence number. Go ask your father, or look it up on Wikipedia.

and methods. They are meant to give you a mechanism to describe what these constructs do, not how they do it. This doesn't mean that you can't include documentation comments inside the body of method, but if you do, those comments will be interpreted as standard block comments and ignored by the Javadoc tool.

There are also files that contain nothing but documentation comments. Every package can contain a special file that can be used to document the overall structure of that package. Known as package comment files, these should be placed at the root of the package. Prior to Java 5.0, these files were named *package.html*; since Java 5.0, you can also use the filename *package-info.java*.

The Javadoc tool is the program that turns your comments into HTML files. Since the tool creates HTML, you can embed HTML into your comments and have those appear (correctly) in the pages generated by the Javadoc tool. This means that all of the formatting mechanisms that are contained in HTML can be used to write your documentation inside your source code. This also means that, if you want to, you can include videos or entire websites in your documentation. Good taste, and the knowledge that your coworkers might be able to find you, should dictate restraint in using such features.

There are also special *tags* that can be used within a documentation comment that the tool will use to create links within the generated documentation. For example, if you need to refer to another class in your documentation, you can enter {@link packagename#classname} and a link to that class's documentation will be inserted in the generated document. You can do the same thing with an interface, using {@link packagename#interfacename}. Other tags can be used for everything from the name of the author of the code to the parameters, return values, and exceptions for a method. One of the more useful tags is {@inheritDoc}, which allows you to inherit the documentation comments from the nearest relative in the type hierarchy. We will see how this works later, but it saves immense amounts of copying and much of the pain of keeping documentation consistent over a system.

The end result of properly written documentation comments run through the Javadoc tool is a set of web pages that act as online documentation for your system. The documentation uses all of the hypertext capabilities inherent in the Web, allowing readers to traverse from one class or interface to another. Even better, most IDEs (which, once again, mostly means both Eclipse and Netbeans) will now display the documentation comments for code that is being used by a programmer as part of their online documentation. So by writing good documentation comments, we not only get better browser-enabled documentation but online, IDE-accessible documentation as well. All colocated with the source code. Such a deal.

Properly written javadoc encourages and supports good object-oriented hygiene in a number of ways. Good javadoc supplies API documentation that can be shipped (and viewed) separately from the implementation of the API, encouraging users of the code to rely only on the documented features and not on implementation details. Good javadoc will specify the semantics of an interface in the documentation for that interface, and will use the documentation for the classes that implement the interface to discuss only the features of that implementation. Indeed, a good rule of system development is to write the javadoc for the interfaces first, and then use that documentation as a form of specification for any classes that implement the interface.

An Example

Rather than trying to give a full tutorial on the capabilities of Javadoc (which can be found at *http://java.sun.com/j2se/1.5.0/docs/tooldocs/windows/javadoc.html*), let's look at an example. One of the places where it is important to fully document our code is when we declare an interface, since it is the documentation that will tell those implementing or using that interface what the intended semantics are. So let's take a look at our Player interface:

```java
package org.oreilly.javaGoodParts.examples.statistics;

import java.util.UUID;
/**
 *Basic interface for a player object.
 */
public interface Player {

    enum Position {
        Pitcher, Catcher, FirstBase, SecondBase,
        ThirdBase, ShortStop, LeftField, CenterField,
        RightField, DH, Utility
    }

    /**
     * Return the identifier for the player. This is just
     * a <code>UUID</code>, generated when the player object is
     * first created, used to distinguish between players
     * that might have the same name.
     */
    UUID getId();

    /**
     * Return the name of the player, as a <code>String</code>
     */
    String getName();

    /**
     * Return a <code>String</code> that is the name of the
     * team for this player.
     */
    Team getTeam();

    /**
     * Return the <code>Position</code> played by this player
     * @return the <code>Position</code> of this player,
     * which will be used to determine the roles that the
     * player has.
```

```
    */
    Position getPosition();

    /**
     * Set the <code>Position</code> of the player
     * @param pos the <code>Position</code> played
     * by this player.
     */
    void setPosition(Position pos);
}
```

The good news here is that there is some documentation that Javadoc can format. The interface has a comment on the purpose of the interface, and each method has a line or two stating what that method does. There is even the HTML markup to visually distinguish the parts of the comment that should be understood as references to code from those that are not. For one of the methods with a return value, an @return tag is specified, and for the method with an argument, the @param tag is specified.

The document produced by the Javadoc tool from this small amount of source is fairly impressive. It will have a summary of the interface, taken from the first line of the doc comment prior to the declaration of the interface. It will list all of the methods, with their signature and a one-line summary of what the method does, again taken from the first line of the doc comment. Finally, each of the methods will be separately documented, using all of the information in the doc comment for that method, including links to the parameters and return value classes. Note that the first line of a documentation comment for a class, interface, or method is automatically used as the summary documentation, so that line should carefully encapsulate the important aspects of the documentation. In javadoc, as in so much else in life, first impressions are important.

What we have in the example is a lot better than much of the documentation that I have seen, which often is either the name of the function and the names of the parameters and return values or the even more common "tbd." But there is a lot more that can, and should, be done.

Let's start at the top. Saying that this is the basic interface for the Player object is true, but not particularly informative. Why do we have a Player interface, rather than relying on the previous interfaces that we defined, such as Batter and Fielder? How will the player object be used? The documentation that we have supplied is fine for the summary of the class, but it doesn't do much to fill in details beyond the summary.

A much better summary of the interface would look something like:

```
/**
 * Basic interface for a player object. An object implementing
 * this interface can be made part of a {@link Team}. Classes
 * implementing this interface will also allow access to statistics
 * gathered for the player in the form of objects of type
 * {@link Batter}, {@link Fielder}, or {@link Catcher}. Which
 * of these roles will be had by a Player will in part be determined
 * by the {@link Position} of the Player.
 */
```

This lets us relate the `Player` object to the objects that will contain them (the `Team` objects). It also says how the interface relates to some of the other interfaces that we have defined in our statistics package, pointing out that `Player` objects can be used to get instances of objects that implement the `Batter`, `Fielder`, or `Catcher` interfaces, depending on the value of the `Position` contained in the `Player` object. This is only a few more lines and didn't take that long to write, but now we can relate our `Player` interface to the other interfaces that we have defined, and the reader can get an understanding of how the `Player` interface will be used.

There are a lot of other things that could go into documenting the interface. We could talk about the invariants that need to be met by any implementation of the interface. We could specify the locking protocols followed, assumed, or required. We could specify the expected life cycle of objects that implement the interface. And we could give a description of how clients might use objects that support the interface.

Now let's take a look at the documentation comments for the various methods. Although it is nice that we have indicated the programming language constructs by putting them into a code font (using HTML), it would be better if we used the javadoc `{@link }` construct to not only show that these are references to Java types but to actually link to those types. While looking at this, we can also see that the doc comments for the `getTeam()` method don't correspond to the signature of the method itself; it looks like this was left over from an earlier design of the interface that would have identified `Team` objects by their `String` names.

Nor is there any discussion of the requirements on the various methods. For example, the existing documentation tells us that the `UUID` returned by the `getId()` method is used to differentiate between players who might have the same name. From this we can conclude that different players should have different IDs, but what is the scope of the difference? Should all players have different IDs, or is it only important that players with the same name have different IDs? This sort of thing might be obvious to the designer of the interface, but for those who are going to use the interface, it might not be so obvious.

Finally, the `Position` enumeration we have defined inside of the `Player` interface has no documentation at all. Given that our expanded summary of the interface tells us that the other interfaces for the statistics package that will be implemented by an object representing a player will depend on the value of the `Position` field for the player, it is important that we document this enumeration. Indeed, as part of that documentation, we might point out that the position of `DH` can be assigned only to `Player` objects that are on a `Team` in the American League, at which point we will realize that we have no information on which league a `Team` is part of in the `Team` interface. By doing the documentation right, we have found a flaw in our design that we can repair before writing the code.

And what about our claim in the summary that an object implementing the `Player` interface can be used to get the various forms of statistics for the player? How does the interface allow this to happen? Maybe we are assuming that objects that implement the `Player` interface will also implement the other statistical interfaces. But in fact (and for reasons that will be discussed later) we have in mind a design that will let an object implementing the statistical interfaces be obtained from an object that implements the `Player` interface. But there is no method that would allow this, so we'd better add one. Writing the documentation not only let us find a flaw in our design, it also allowed us to see where our design was incomplete.

If we make all of these changes, then the result looks more like:

```java
package org.oreilly.javaGoodParts.examples.statistics;

import java.util.UUID;

/**
 * Basic interface for a player object. An object implementing
 * this interface can be made part of a {@link Team}. Classes
 * implementing this interface will also allow access to statistics
 * gathered for the player in the form of objects of type
 * {@link Batter}, {@link Fielder}, or {@link Catcher}. Which
 * of these roles will be had by a Player will in part be determined
 * by the {@link Position} of the Player.
 */
public interface Player {

    /**
     * The position played by the player. The position can be used to determine
     * what objects supporting other interfaces will be returned by an
     * implementation of the object that also implements this interface. All
     * objects that implement this interface that are not assigned a Position of
     * <code> Pitcher</code> and are not on {@link Team} in the American League
     * will return an object implementing the {@link Batter} interface. All
     * objects that implement this interface will return an object implement the
     * {@link Fielder} interface except for those that have a position of
     * <code>DH</code>; only players on a {@link Team} that is in the American
     * League can be assigned that position. Only players assigned the position
     * of <code> Catcher</code> will return an object implementing the
     * {@link Catcher} interface.
     */
    enum Position {
        Pitcher, Catcher, FirstBase, SecondBase,
        ThirdBase, ShortStop, LeftField, CenterField,
        RightField, DH, Utility
    }

    /**
     * Return the identifier for the player. This is just
     * a {@link UUID}, generated when the player object is
     * first created, used to distinguish between players
     * that might have the same name. It is up to the
     * implementation of the method to ensure that the
     * identifier is unique over the set of all players.
```

```
 *
 * @return A {@link UUID} that uniquely identifies this player
 */
UUID getId();

/**
 * Return the name of the player, as a {@link String}
 *
 * @return A {@link String} that is the name of this player
 */
String getName();

/**
 * Return a {@link Team} object that represents
 * the team that this player is on.
 *
 * @return The {@link Team} for which this player plays
 */
Team getTeam();

/**
 * Return the {@link Position} played by this player,
 * which can be used to determine the roles that
 * the player has.
 * @return the {@link Position} of this player
 */
Position getPosition();

/**
 * Set the {@link Position} of the player.
 *
 * @param pos the {@link Position} played
 * by this player
 */
void setPosition(Position pos);

/**
 * Return a {@link Batter} object if this player has the role of a
 * Batter, otherwise returns null.
 *
 * @return a {@link Batter} object containing the batting statistics
 * for this player.
 */
Batter asBatter();
...
}
```

This gives a more complete idea of how the interface is supposed to be used, and what the requirements are for implementations of the interface. We have not completed the interface yet; there is only a single method to return a statistical object. There will need to be parallel methods that return the other statistical objects added to the interface, a task we will turn to later.

The `@link` tag allows us to form a web link in our documentation, enabling the reader to navigate to the related entries through the browser. But that isn't the only form of link that we can have in our documentation. Since any valid HTML can also be used, we can include links to outside documents, websites, or even videos. This ability should be used judiciously (after all, this is documentation that is meant to be read online by developers; they are trying to get a job done, not reading for recreation). But here it might make sense to include references to the definitions of some of the more obscure batting or fielding statistics in the documentation for our `Batter` or `Fielder` interfaces. For example, we might want to change our documentation comment for the `getOBP()` method to something like:

```
/**
 * Returns the on-base percentage for this hitter,
 * <a href="http://en.wikipedia.org/wiki/On_base_percentage">defined</a>
 * as (hits + walks)/at-bats
 * @return the on-base percentage
 * @throws NotEnoughAtBatsException if the number of at-bats, walks,
 * and sacrifices is insufficient to establish a meaningful on-base
 * percentage
 */
```

which includes a link to the Wikipedia article that gives the definition of on-base percentage. This sort of thing can be taken to extremes pretty easily, but it is a capability that, if used occasionally, can make your documentation much clearer than it would be without the outside references.

Implementation Documentation

Thus far, we have been looking mostly at the javadoc for interfaces. The documentation for an interface can be thought of as a specification for any class that implements that interface. But what about the classes themselves? Do they need the same kind of javadoc?

If you don't do anything (that is, if you don't write any documentation comments for an implementation class), a class that implements an interface will inherit the documentation from the interface that it implements. The documentation will show this, with the Javadoc tool inserting the phrase "Description copied from interface:" and the interface name at the beginning of the description. At worst, you will get the specification of the method in the implementation class. But we can do a lot better than that.

The first thing that we can do better is to use the `{@inheritDoc}` tag to get the documentation contents of the closest ancestor in the inheritance hierarchy. In our simple example, this is the same as letting the interface documentation be copied in, with the only visible difference being that the comment "Description copied from interface:" is not inserted. But if we start inheriting the implementation as well as just the interface, the difference is important. Inheriting the documentation will now cause any implementation comments on the superclass to be brought into the documentation on the new class, rather than just the documentation of the interface. Using the {@inheritDoc} tag is a good habit to get into.

For example, consider the method getId in the Player interface. The documentation comment for the Player interface tells us that this method should return the ID for the player. We know that the ID should be unique over the set of all players, but it would be nice to know how the implementation ensures this. One alternative would be to have the javadoc for the method in the PlayerImpl say something like:

```
/**
 * This implementation will generate a player
 * id by using the standard {@link UUID#randomUUID}
 * generator for UUIDs, which is a cryptographically
 * strong UUID. This should guarantee enough
 * uniqueness for this application.
 * @return the UUID that is the player id
 */
```

This is helpful, but in doing this, we lose the documentation for the method that we wrote for the interface. We could always put a pointer to the interface somewhere in the implementation documentation, but then we will have the user of the documentation jumping from entry to entry in the document, which can be annoying (and error-prone). A better solution is to inherit the documentation from the interface, and then augment that documentation with details about this implementation of the interface. We can use the {@inheritDoc} tag for this, and consequently we will get a better form of documentation, which looks like:

```
/**
 * {@inheritDoc }
 * <p>
 * This implementation will generate a player
 * id by using the standard {@link UUID#randomUUID}
 * generator for UUIDs, which is a cryptographically
 * strong UUID. This should guarantee enough
 * uniqueness for this application.
 * @return the UUID that is the player id
 */
```

By adding the {@inheritDoc} tag, we get the documentation for the interface included in our documentation for the implementation. We can then go on to talk about the details of this particular implementation. Note the use of the HTML tag <p> to indicate a paragraph break. If we didn't include this, the inherited documentation would be in the same paragraph as the documentation for the implementation, which is less visually appealing and could lead to confusion.

Package Documentation

We've taken a look at how to use Javadoc to document interfaces and implementations. This generates a lot of useful documentation when used correctly, and the nice thing about the documentation is that it is colocated with the code that it is describing, making it that much harder to change one without changing the other. Of course, programmers in a hurry (or those who hate to write anything that isn't compiled) will still avoid writing documentation, or revising it when needed, but javadoc makes it more convenient to do the right thing and make sure that changes in the code get described in the documentation.

If this were all that javadoc did, it would be a good thing. Indeed, this is all that most programmers use javadoc to do. But there is a missing piece of the documentation if all that is described are the interfaces and classes. What hasn't been shown yet is how all of those pieces are meant to fit together to form a system. This is the architecture of the system, and it provides a framework for the reader of the documentation to put the pieces into place and see the system as a system. Although the individual class and interface entries may tell the reader how the pieces function individually, it is this broader documentation that tells the reader the structure that unifies those pieces.

Javadoc supplies a mechanism for this kind of architectural documentation, which is (unfortunately) often either unknown, ignored, or abused. This mechanism is the package comment file, which I mentioned earlier in this chapter. In any package, you can include a file that can be used to specify the architectural documentation for the package. Prior to JDK 5.0, this file was named *package.html*, and was a standard HTML file that could contain documentation about the package. Since JDK 5.0, this file can be a java source file containing the package declaration, package annotations, and the documentation (including all of the standard javadoc tags).

Such comment files need not be huge. For example, a reasonable comment for our statistics package might look something like:

```
/**
 * Provides the interfaces needed to build a system
 * that tracks the statistics of a group of baseball
 * players.<p>
 *
 * The statistics for individuals are tracked through
 * an object that implements the {@link
 * org.oreilly.javaGoodParts.examples.statistics.Player}
 * interface. A player will have a {@link
 * org.oreilly.javaGoodParts.examples.statistics.Player.Position},
 * and based on that position will implement the
 * interfaces that track statistics for the various
 * roles that player may have. Players are
 * grouped together in objects that implement the
 * {@link org.oreilly.javaGoodParts.examples.statistics.Team}
 * interface.<p>
 *
 * Objects that implement the {@link
 * org.oreilly.javaGoodParts.examples.statistics.Player}
 * interface will implement calls that return the statistics
 * interfaces, such as the {@link
 * org.oreilly.javaGoodParts.examples.statistics.Batter}
 * interface. The current Player interface only reflects the
 * ability to return a {@link org.oreilly.javaGoodParts.examples.statistics.Batter}
```

```
 * interface, but the ability to return other statistical interfaces will
 * be added later in the development of this example.
 * <p>
 *
 * Only players that have the position <code>Catcher</code>
 * will return an object that implements the {@link
 * org.oreilly.javaGoodParts.examples.statistics.Catcher}
 * interface, as this allows tracking statistics that are
 * unique to that position.<p>
 *
 * At this time there is no interface that can be
 * used to track pitching statistics, as this is an
 * example system and pitching statistics get arbitrarily
 * complex. However, it should be clear from the
 * various other interfaces what such a <code>
 * Pitcher</code> interface would look like.
package org.oreilly.javaGoodParts.examples.statistics;
```

This comment will appear as part of the documentation for the overall package. Although it is just a couple of paragraphs, it clearly states the intention for each of the interfaces, how they are meant to be fit together, and how the package might be extended for more functionality (and why it wasn't extended in that way originally). For a programmer coming into the package for the first time, it shows the overall structure and gives the newcomer a foothold on the various pieces.

One thing to notice about the *package-info.java* file is that links need to use the fully qualified class or interface name. This is because of an interesting catch-22 of such files. Document comments are only processed before a declaration. The only declaration that can appear in a *package-info.java* file is the declaration of the package. So the document comments need to appear before the declaration of the package so that the tool generating the documentation will read it. But prior to the package declaration, there is no reference package for the links. So you need to put in the fully qualified name of the class or interface. This is something of a hassle, but is worth it to get some general description of the interaction of those package pieces into the documentation.

Style Guides, Editors, and Nonterminating Discussions

Over the years, there have been lots of discussions of what *proper* document comments should look like. Various groups have issued style guides. Perhaps the best known of these guides is "How to Write Doc Comments for the Javadoc Tool" (*http://java.sun .com/j2se/javadoc/writingdoccomments*), which goes into mind-numbing detail on how these comments should be written. It covers everything from which person to use (third) to the length of the lines of your comments (80, showing that the influence of punch cards will never die).

Now, I have no general objections to standards, either for documentation comments or for source code. Every organization should have some style guide, to ensure that practices that can lead to errors are avoided and help give uniformity to the work that comes out of the organization. More importantly, it helps those who have to maintain the documentation (and the code) when they need to plunge into what you have written and make changes in the future.

But like coding conventions, documentation conventions should be considered as guidelines, not as inflexible rules. Finding a set of guides that work for your organization is a good exercise, but doing so will almost certainly mean that some members of the staff will want to control things that seem way too minor to worry about. A sense of proportion is needed in such discussions, but rarely found. My experience has been that discussions of documentation conventions soon become similar to discussions about coding conventions or which editor is superior. They don't end.

This is where editors or technical writers can make a huge difference to a group, even when those editors or technical writers are other members of the programming staff. Having a second person read over your comments can be just as important as having someone else read over and review your code (and we all do that, right?). If the editor has trouble understanding your documentation, then other readers will have trouble, too. Establishing a review process that includes the documentation will help the organization and improve your comments. It may seem to take longer, but it is one of those things that will save huge amounts of time in the long run (where the long run is actually shorter than the time spent on the overall project). It is also an indication, and perhaps the output, of a conscious design process for the system being documented. Good design is hard, and often describing a design is a necessary part in making the beginnings of a design mature. Writing the javadoc can be an aid in this maturation, and can help others understand why the system is the way it is.

CHAPTER 8
Collections

Hierarchy is basic to what we do as programmers. We build large programs by breaking them into interacting pieces that are each smaller and simpler than the whole program. We break those pieces into still smaller and simpler parts, until we get to something small enough and simple enough to be understood and implemented. In the same way, we build up the information in a program by collecting together information. Bits are assembled into bytes and sequences of bytes that can be interpreted as characters, numbers, or strings. We group this data together with some code to make objects, the basic piece of abstraction in object-oriented programming languages such as Java. But we don't stop there; we collect objects together in other objects, building more and more complex structures.

Not long ago much of a programmer's time was spent in building up these larger structures. If you wanted a list of some kind of object, you built your own list. If you wanted a set, you built a set. Much of the basic curriculum of a computer science education was (and, in many places, still is) given over to teaching how to build such data structures.

The Java environment, fortunately, frees programmers from this level of building. The Java libraries contain a selection of implementations of collections that include nearly any grouping mechanism one might need. This collections library, found in the package `java.util`, can save a programmer so much time and effort that it is definitely worth including in the good parts of the language. However, though it is a great time and effort saver, it also has some quirks that need to be known. So we will now turn our attention to the collections.

The Basics

We have already mentioned a place where the Java collections will prove useful. Remember in Chapter 7 when we were talking about putting groups of players together into a team? We didn't actually formalize this notion in any code, so I will turn to that task now. The first thing to do is to decide what the interface to such a Team might look like. As a first candidate, I will propose something along the lines of:

```java
package org.oreilly.javaGoodParts.examples.statistics;

import java.util.List;
/**
 * The <code>Team</code> interface, which defines
 * the notion of a team for our statistics package. A
 * team is, at first incarnation, simply a collection of
 * players. All teams have a name.
 */
public interface Team {
    /**
     * Return a <code>String</code> that is the name of
     * this team.
     */
    String getName();

    /**
     * Return a list of the players that are on this
     * team.
     */
    List getPlayerList();

    /**
     * Add a player to the team.
     */
    void addPlayer(Player toAdd);

    /**
     * Remove a player from the team.
     */
    void removePlayer(Player toRemove);
}
```

We see that one of the methods in the interface, getPlayerList(), returns a List object. This is a type that is defined in the java.util package, and as the name implies, it provides us a higher-level construct that is made up of other objects. As of Java 1.5, we would declare this somewhat differently, but we are going to start simple, and get more complex a bit later in this chapter.

The java.util package is itself a rather strange beast. The package name util is about as uninformative as you can get; it could just as easily have been called stuff or other or doesNotFitAnywhereElse. Indeed, this package contains a motley group of interfaces, classes, and exceptions for such things as the system random number generator, a string tokenizer, an event model, and some internationalization tools. But this package also contains a set of collection interfaces and implementations that, when properly understood and used, can save a programmer a huge amount of time and effort.

The List interface allows us to add Player objects to the team, remove Players, and iterate through the group of players. If we add a Player object to a list that is already full, the List will automatically resize. We can control where in the list a Player object is added, or we can just use the default and add a player to the end of the list. A List also allows the same Player object to be inserted into the List multiple times; if we do that, removing a player will still leave some copies of the Player object in the list, and iterating through the list will give us multiple instances of that Player. In fact, the List acts a lot like an array of player objects, but frees us from having to do much of the maintenance of the array (such as resizing or moving entries around) when we want to insert an entry in a particular place. And that's the idea: the collections are here to free us from writing code.

But the fact that we can insert the same Player object into a List multiple times and end up with multiple occurrences of that Player object on the Team doesn't seem right. After all, the same player can be on a team only once, at least at any one time. What we really want is for the Team to contain some way of storing all of the Players on the team so that we are guaranteed that no Player can be inserted twice on the same Team (or remain after being removed).

We could do this by adding our own checks to the addPlayer() and removePlayer() methods. We could, for example, begin the addPlayer() method with a check to see whether the Player being inserted was already in the List and simply return the answer. Even though this should keep any duplicate Player objects out of the List, we will also add some code to our removePlayer() method to ensure that multiple copies of any Player object will be removed when that method is called. The resulting (first) implementation of a class that implements the Team interface might look something like:

```
package org.oreilly.javaGoodParts.examples.impl;

import java.util.ArrayList;
import java.util.List;
import org.oreilly.javaGoodParts.examples.statistics.Player;
import org.oreilly.javaGoodParts.examples.statistics.Team;

/**
 * A first implementation of the Team interface, using
 * an ArrayList as the backing store for the Players on
 * the team.
 */
public class TeamImpl implements Team {
    private String name;
    private ArrayList players = new ArrayList();

    /**
     * Create a TeamImpl object, with the name
     * supplied.
     */
    public TeamImpl(String teamName){
        name = teamName;
    }
```

```
/**
 * Return a <code>String</code> that is the name of
 * this team.
 */
public String getName(){
    return name;
}
/**
 * Return a list of the players that are on this
 * team.
 */
public List getPlayerList(){
    return players;
}
/**
 * Add a player to the team.
 */
public void addPlayer(Player toAdd){
    if (players.contains(toAdd)){
        return;
    }
    players.add(toAdd);
}
/**
 * Remove a player from the team.
 */
public void removePlayer(Player toRemove){
    while (players.contains(toRemove)){
        players.remove(toRemove);
    }
}
}
```

Note that we have used the ArrayList class to store the Player objects on the Team. An ArrayList is an implementation of the List interface, using an array as the backing store. It handles all of the issues around using an array, such as resizing, shuffling, and constructing an iterator over the array. We could have done this ourselves, but using the existing code means that we don't have to write the code ourselves. Further, the existing code is tested, debugged, and probably runs at least as fast as the code we would have written (and, very likely, runs faster).

But there is a better way. Although we have collected the Player objects using a List, we really don't want the semantics of a List. We would really like a collection that allows a Player to be in the collection only once. And there is such an interface and implementation in the collection classes: the Set. Looking at the javadoc, we can see that a Set is a collection in which no element can occur multiple times. Unlike a List, a Set does not guarantee the order of the elements stored in it when you iterate over the Set. But we aren't going to depend on the order of our Player objects in such an iteration, so the Set seems to fit the bill nicely.

The first thing we need to do is change our Team interface, removing the List that is returned from the getPlayerList() method and returning a Set instead. While we are doing that, we will change the name of the method to better reflect what is being returned. The result will look something like:

```
package org.oreilly.javaGoodParts.examples.statistics;

import java.util.Set;

/**
 * The <code>Team</code> interface, which defines
 * the notion of a team for our statistics package. A
 * team is, at first incarnation, simply a collection of
 * players. All teams have a name.
 */
public interface Team {

    /**
     * Return a <code>String</code> that is the name of
     * this team.
     */
    String getName();

    /**
     * Return the players that are on this
     * team.
     */
    Set getRoster();

    /**
     * Add a player to the team.
     */
    void addPlayer(Player toAdd);

    /**
     * Remove a player from the team.
     */
    void removePlayer(Player toRemove);
}
```

Having changed the name of the method that gets us the `Player` objects that are on the team and the return type for that method, we now need to change our `PlayerImpl` to reflect the change in the interface. If we check the javadoc for the `Set` interface, we will find a number of classes that implement that interface. Most of these implementations are for special sets of a particular type, but the `HashSet` will do nicely for our uses. As the name implies, a `HashSet` implements the `Set` interface using a hash table as a backing store. The nice thing is, we don't have to care. All we want is an implementation of the `Set` interface that we can use, and one is supplied. So we can change our `TeamImpl` code to something like:

```
package org.oreilly.javaGoodParts.examples.impl;

import java.util.HashSet;
import java.util.Set;
import org.oreilly.javaGoodParts.examples.statistics.Player;
import org.oreilly.javaGoodParts.examples.statistics.Team;
```

```
/**
 * A second implementation of the Team interface, using
 * a HashSet as the backing store for the Players on
 * the team, after the interface has been changed to
 * return a Set from the getPlayers() method.
 */
public class TeamImpl implements Team {

    private String name;
    private HashSet players = new HashSet();

    /**
     * Create a TeamImpl object, with the name
     * supplied.
     */
    public TeamImpl(String teamName) {
        name = teamName;
    }

    /**
     * Return a <code>String</code> that is the name of
     * this team.
     */
    public String getName() {
        return name;
    }

    /**
     * Return a list of the players that are on this
     * team.
     */
    public Set getRoster() {
        return new HashSet(players);
    }

    /**
     * Add a player to the team.
     */
    public void addPlayer(Player toAdd) {
        players.add(toAdd);
    }

    /**
     * Remove a player from the team.
     */
    public void removePlayer(Player toRemove) {
    players.remove(toRemove);
    }
}
```

Note that this simplifies the implementations of our **addPlayer()** and **removePlayer()** methods. We no longer need to check for duplicates, because this is done for us in the **HashSet** implementation.

Note that since our methods `addPlayer()` and `removePlayer()` only use methods on a `Set`, we could have declared our private `players` variable simply as a `Set` rather than as a `HashSet`. This would show that we depend only on the interface for a `Set` rather than on a particular implementation of the `Set`. However, we still need to create a concrete instance of the `Set` somewhere. We could have some kind of factory method, perhaps controlled by some property, that would determine at runtime what particular instantiation of the `Set` interface we would use. But for the purposes of this example, we will tie the implementation of our `Player` interface to an implementation of the `Set` interface, and create the `HashSet` directly in our `PlayerImpl` class.

Also note that what is returned from the method `getRoster()` is not a reference to the private `players` field, but a new `HashSet` that is initialized with the contents of that private field. This ensures that no one can manipulate the contents of the `TeamImpl` object's copy of the roster. This approach, which tries to return copies of private data rather than references to that private data, is generally a good idea. Since Java has garbage collection, we don't even have to worry about this creating a memory leak. Although there are some performance implications, they are generally small and worth the added guarantees of correctness.

To use the objects in a collection like a `Set`, we can get an `Iterator`. An `Iterator` is a special object that has a very simple interface. In its basic form, an `Iterator` contains only the methods `hasNext()`, `next()`, and `remove()`. But since most of what we want to do is go through the objects in a collection (and know when we are done with that), these suffice.

For example, suppose we wanted to add a method to our `Formatter` object that would print out the roster for a team. We would like to print out the name of the `Team`, and then print out the names of the players on that team below, one per line, properly indented. To do this, we would add the method:

```
public static void FormatRoster(Team toFormat){
        Player p;
        System.out.println(toFormat.getName());
        Iterator e = toFormat.getRoster().iterator();
        while (e.hasNext()){
            p = (Player)e.next();
            System.out.println("\t" + p.getName());
        }
    }
```

Up to the release of Java 1.5, this is all that you needed to know about the collections. They were a set of interfaces and implementations that added most of the usual ways of gathering objects together to the standard libraries. Using them was simple, easy, and saved everyone a lot of time. But all that changed with Java 1.5 and the introduction of parameterized types. This was a general change to the language, but the greatest impact with respect to the libraries occurs in the collections. If you are not using a version of Java beyond 1.4, you can stop reading this chapter now. But for the rest of you (and I'm assuming that this is just about everyone), let's continue on to see what parameterized types and generics are and what they do to the collections.

Parameterized Types

The motivation for the introduction of parameterized types can be seen in our last example, when we were using our Set of Players to print out a team roster. As we iterated through the Set of Player objects on a team, we had to perform a class cast on the object returned from the hasNext() method, as seen in the line:

```
p = (Player)e.next();
```

This is, in some sense, an unsafe operation. Even though the only way we know of to put an object into the List that is return from the getRoster() method on a Team object is to call the addPlayer() method on the Team object, and even though the type of object that is passed in to the addPlayer() method is checked, it is certainly logically possible that something other than a Player object can be inserted into the List, perhaps in some method we know nothing about. Certainly, if the getRoster() method returned a reference to the players field rather than a copy, we would have no guarantees of what had been inserted into the Set. And if an object that is not a Player is inserted into the List, the casting of the result of the next() operation on the iterator will fail.

Of course, there are mechanisms in Java that would let us write code to deal with the failure. We could check, before the cast, to make sure that the object returned from the iterator was actually an instanceof the Player type. And the cast operation in the Java language is checked. This means that unlike casting in C or C++, where a cast in an assertion that the area of memory referred to should be treated as a particular data type (whether it is or not), an attempt to cast an object in Java into some type different from the object's true type results in throwing a Runtime exception. If no one catches this exception, then the program will terminate, but this is a very different failure than what one would get in a language where a cast is an assertion; in those languages, the program will merrily continue, but the result of the cast will be garbage. In those languages, the result of such a cast will generally not appear until your program has run merrily along for some time, and will cause it to crash far away from the original source of the problem—if you are lucky, that is. If you are not (and none of us are in the long run; that's why we're programmers), then the result of such a cast will be data corruption that won't be caught until some completely different program fails in an utterly inexplicable way.

So, if we wanted to be really paranoid and careful about ensuring that we never caused the program to fail because something that didn't support the Player interface crept into our Set of Player objects in a Team, we could have written our FormatRoster() method like this:

```
public static void FormatRoster(Team toFormat){
        Player p;
        Object o;
```

```
                System.out.println(toFormat.getName());
                Iterator e = toFormat.getRoster().iterator();
                while (e.hasNext()){
                    o = e.next();
                    if (o instanceof Player){
                        try{
                            p = (Player)o;
                            System.out.println("\t" + p.getName());
                        } catch (ClassCastException ex){
                            e.remove();
                        }
                    } else {
                        e.remove();
                    }
                }
        }
```

On this approach, we extract an `Object` from the `Set` using our `Iterator`, knowing that the contents must be at least that. We then check to see whether the object that we got is an `instanceof` the `Player` type; if it is not ,we will simply remove it from the list. Only then do we cast, but being fully paranoid, we wrap our cast in a **try** block, so that if it fails, we will catch the `ClassCastException` and, once again, remove the offending object from the list. With both the belt and the suspenders, we can be sure that we will catch any offending object that has been misplaced into our collection of `Player` objects.

The worry about this approach is that, even though it is safe, the safety is provided at runtime. What was desired was some mechanism that could be used to ensure that the collections were used safely at compile time. And thus was born Java Generics, or parameterized types.

I'm not going to try to give a full tutorial on the use of generics in Java here. The subject has been covered elsewhere, and a full exposition would take up more space than warranted in this book. What follows is an attempt to give a good working knowledge of the simplest way of using generics, especially with the collection classes.

The idea behind generics is reasonably simple, although the details seem to get arbitrarily complex. The simple idea is that we can have variables in some declarations that vary over types rather than instances of types. We can then instantiate particular versions of these generically declared items by binding the type variable to some particular value. The value of having a variable in the declaration is that it allows us to write code that can deal with all of the particular instantiations of the type variable to real types.

OK, maybe that last paragraph didn't help. Actually, the best way to get a feel for generics is to look at how the introduction of generics changed the collection classes. Which shouldn't be a surprise, since the collections were really the reason that generics were introduced into the language in the first place.

With the introduction of generics, collections such as a `Set` can now be declared using a type parameter. Syntactically, such a parameter follows the type name and is enclosed by brackets. So now, instead of saying that the return value from the `getRoster()`

method of our Team interface is a Set, we can declare it a Set<Player>, or a set of Player objects.

If we look at the documentation for the Set interface, we can see that what is documented is Set<E>. E, in this case, is a type parameter that is used throughout the documentation (and the definition of the interface). Not only does the declaration of something that is a Set use this parameter, but the parameter is used in the declaration of the methods of the interface. In particular, the method used to place an object into the collection is now declared as:

```
boolean add(E e)
```

and the method that gives us an iterator is now declared as:

```
Iterator<E> iterator()
```

This means that when we declare a Set of a particular type, that type will be used to replace all of the instances of the type variable E in the definition. So by returning a Set<Player> from getRoster(), we assure that only a Player object can be added to the Set, and the Iterator that is returned from the iterator() method on that Set will give us only Player objects. We don't have to cast the result of using the iterator, and the compiler can check all of these guarantees.

To see how this works in practice, let's go back to our baseball statistics package. We start by changing the Team interface so that the return value of getRoster() uses generics, adding a type parameter to the return type:

```
package org.oreilly.javaGoodParts.examples.statistics;

import java.util.Set;

/**
 * The <code>Team</code> interface, which defines
 * the notion of a team for our statistics package. A
 * team is, at first incarnation, simply a collection of
 * players. All teams have a name.
 */
public interface Team {

    /**
     * Return a <code>String</code> that is the name of
     * this team.
     */
    String getName();

    /**
     * Return the players that are on this
     * team. The set returned is a set of player
     * objects.
     */
    Set<Player> getRoster();

    /**
     * Add a player to the team.
```

```
    */
    void addPlayer(Player toAdd);

    /**
     * Remove a player from the team.
     */
    void removePlayer(Player toRemove);
}
```

We now change the implementation class we have for this interface to use a parameterized version of the HashSet class that matches the version used in the interface:

```
package org.oreilly.javaGoodParts.examples.impl;

import java.util.HashSet;
import java.util.Set;
import org.oreilly.javaGoodParts.examples.statistics.Player;
import org.oreilly.javaGoodParts.examples.statistics.Team;

/**
 * A third implementation of the Team interface, using
 * a HashSet as the backing store for the Players on
 * the team, after the interface has been changed to
 * return a Set from the getPlayers() method.
 */
public class TeamImpl implements Team {

    private String name;
    private HashSet<Player> players = new HashSet<Player>();

    /**
     * Create a TeamImpl object, with the name
     * supplied.
     */
    public TeamImpl(String teamName) {
        name = teamName;
    }

    /**
     * Return a <code>String</code> that is the name of
     * this team.
     */
    public String getName() {
        return name;
    }

    /**
     * Return a list of the players that are on this
     * team.
     */
    public Set<Player>  getRoster() {
        return players;
    }

    /**
     * Add a player to the team.
```

```
    */
    public void addPlayer(Player toAdd) {
        players.add(toAdd);
    }

    /**
     * Remove a player from the team.
     */
    public void removePlayer(Player toRemove) {
            players.remove(toRemove);
    }
}
```

Now we can change the method that prints out the roster for a team, simplifying it considerably. We no longer need to check to see that the objects returned from the Set obtained by calling getRoster() are players, since that has been ensured by the parameterized versions of the collections that we are using. We also don't have to do the casting to the Player type. So now our FormatRoster() method can look like:

```
public static void FormatRoster(Team toFormat){
    System.out.println(toFormat.getName());
    Iterator<Player> e = toFormat.getRoster().iterator();
    while (e.hasNext()){
        System.out.println("\t" + e.next().getName());
    }
}
```

In fact, we can simplify this code even more. The Java language now has a special type of for loop, just for iteration over collections. Instead of the code just shown, we could get the same results with:

```
public static void FormatRoster(Team toFormat){
        System.out.println(toFormat.getName());
        for (Player i : toFormat.getRoster()){
            System.out.println("\t" + i.getName());
        }
}
```

Best of all, we have eliminated all of the code that we had to check to make sure that the types were correct in our collection. Because we were able to specify a type parameter on the collections that we used, we can be sure that all that was put into the collection, and all that will come out, are going to be objects of the right type. There are no casts in our code that could cause a runtime exception to be thrown. So there is no way that this code can go wrong, at least with respect to the types of the objects.

Well, mostly. In fact, the addition of generics and the parameterization of the collections do not eliminate the possibility of having the wrong type of object in such a collection. To understand why requires that we look a little more carefully at how generics were added to the language.

The generics system was designed at a time when there was a prohibition about even thinking about making changes to either the Java virtual machine or the bytecodes understood by that machine. This was in keeping with a number of edicts at the time, but it was mostly a way of ensuring that Java programs written on early versions of the platform ran on later versions of the virtual machine. It is actually sort of amazing that the JVM itself has changed so little over the years. Either through luck or skill, most of the changes have occurred in the libraries, with a smaller set of changes occurring in the language and very little change occurring in the VM itself.

But the inability to change the VM or bytecodes meant that parameterized types could occur only in the source code. The type system of the runtime hasn't changed, and doesn't include generics or parameterized types. What we see in our code as a `Set<Player>` is seen in the bytecodes as simply a `Set` of objects.

In many ways, the fact that the designers of the generics system could do much of anything without involving the runtime is a testament to their skills. The resulting system*uses lots of tricks in the compiler to make sure that the type safety is guaranteed, and has the compiler insert the casts that are needed to change the runtime objects that come from parameterized collections into the correct type.

This has two implications. First, the casting of objects from one type to another is still in the code, even though it is hidden from the programmer. Using generics just means that the compiler will insert the casts into your code rather than you having to write those casts. For those who feel that the whole point of generics is to get away from such casts (because, for some reason, those casts are evil), this is the moral equivalent of purchasing indulgences. Someone else (the compiler) sins so that you don't have to. It hardly seems right.

I'll admit that this objection to generics doesn't really bother me, for the simple reason that I don't think type casting in a language like Java is an indication that your code is somehow faulty. I think this view is a holdover from the attitude that developed in languages like C, where casting did show a weakness in the type system of the language. Of course, since C didn't really have a type system, it isn't surprising that there were weaknesses to it. But I digress.

The other implication, which is more serious, is that type safety for parameterized types can only be ensured over a compilation unit. That means that if you are using code that was compiled elsewhere, you need to trust that whoever it was that wrote that code (even if it was you some time earlier) made sure that all of the uses of parameterized types were safe in their code. If that code was not completely type-safe, you may run into trouble using the code, and you won't know it until the problem happens.

To see an example, let's return to our `TeamImpl` class. We will leave it exactly the way it is, except that we will change the internal representation of the `players` collection from a `HashSet<Player>` to a simple `HashSet`. A collection without a type parameter is perfectly legal, left in to make sure that programs written before generics were added

---

* Those who want details of the way generics were added should see the original design documents, such as *Adding Generics to the Java Programming Language* by Gilad Bracha, et al. (*http://www.cs.purdue.edu/homes/ hosking/352/generics.pdf*).

still work. The code will still compile, although I will get a warning from the compiler like:

```
TeamImpl.java uses unchecked or unsafe operations.
Note: Recompile with -Xlint:unchecked for details.
```

But this is a warning, easy to ignore (and, at times, easy to miss among the other warnings generated by the compiler). I should make the changes to my code that would eliminate the warning, but there are all kinds of things that I should do that I don't get around to doing. Even with the warning, the compiler will generate a class file, and the program will run just fine. Until it doesn't.

If this isn't repaired, then I'm back to the situation where something other than a `Player` object might make it into the collection of players. If there is some other way to access the local collection, or some method that also is missing a type parameter, then most anything could be placed in the `HashSet`. And, as I write the client code that uses the `TeamImpl` class (probably through the `Team` interface), I will never know. Unless I compile the `TeamImpl` class myself along with any code that I write that uses that class (and I might not even have the code), I will never get the warning. But my client code may fail when running. Even worse, it will fail with a `ClassCastException` caused by a cast inserted by the compiler that will point to a place in my client code where, when I look at the source, there is no class cast.

There are other, more obscure places where you can also get into trouble using generics. For example, there are tricks that can be used in object serialization (discussed in Chapter 9) that require casting, since serialization entails converting a series of bits into an object. Most of these problems come down to the lack of runtime support for generics, which makes generics a compile-time system, coupled with the fact that Java is a dynamic environment in which a lot happens at runtime.

When generics were first proposed, there were many who were upset with this mismatch. I was one of them. This is not to say that the design is bad; indeed, given the constraint that the virtual machine could not be changed, the design of generics is intellectually remarkable. But because of the constraints on the design, the design does not fit naturally with the basic nature of the language and environment. So although remarkable, it is not a perfect fit, and the resulting system has some obscure holes.

All that said, after using generics for a couple of years, I think that they do make the language better. While I'm not sure I would include them in the good parts of the language, they certainly get my vote for inclusion into the useful parts of the language. They are useful bits of documentation, and do discover some errors at compile time that would have been revealed only at runtime before generics were added. They are complicated to use in some of their more obscure patterns.[†] But the simple uses are easy to understand and make your code better.

[†] If you really want to get a grasp on how to use generics, you will need to read the generics chapter in Josh Bloch's *Effective Java* (Prentice Hall) a couple of times.

Advanced Topics

Before leaving our discussion of the collections, let's look at a couple of uses of those classes that might not immediately spring to mind when we think about aggregating objects together. As useful as the basic aggregations are, these others can save you even more time, and let you avoid introducing even more bugs into your code.

Thus far, our statistics package has let us collect statistics and put `Player` objects together as `Teams`. But we would like to be able to compare the statistics of the various players. There are two tasks that we will need to do to get to a point where this is possible. The first is to associate the various ways we have of gathering statistics, embodied in our notions of a `Batter`, `Fielder`, and `Catcher`, with our `Player` objects. The second is to come up with some way of sorting those various categories into lists that will allow the comparison.

The first of these, associating the various interfaces and classes we have defined for gathering and reporting the different kinds of statistics with a `Player` object, is often done through the type system by constructing a hierarchy. And we can almost do this, saying that every `Player` is also a `Batter`, and every `Batter` is a `Fielder`. If we took this approach, then we would change our `Batter` interface to begin with:

```
public interface Batter extends Fielder {
```

and our `Player` interface to begin with:

```
public interface Player extends Batter {
```

and change the implementations as well. Thus every `Player` would also be a `Batter` and a `Fielder`, and would support all of the methods needed for the statistics reporting.

But this doesn't really work. To begin with, we still have the `Catcher` interface to insert into the hierarchy, and will someday have to extend the set of classes to include a `Pitcher` interface. In the real world we are trying to represent, all catchers are also fielders and batters, but there are special statistics that apply only to catchers. If we make `Catcher` a superclass of `Player`, we get the "is a" relationship right, but then we have trouble getting from a `Player` object to a `Catcher` interface. Worse still, not all batters are fielders (because of designated hitters). Similarly, if we add pitchers, we will have players who are not batters (at least in the American League), but are fielders.

It is inconvenient when the world doesn't fit our notion of a type system, but it happens. When it does, one thing we could do is simply ignore the world. We could, for example, say that designated hitters are fielders who just never field, or that pitchers in the American League are batters who never get enough plate appearances. Or we could complicate our type hierarchy, introducing special interfaces for American League pitchers and designated hitters, and wedge in catchers someplace or other.

Or we could do the right thing and decide that we can't capture the relationship between the various statistical classes with the type hierarchy. A simpler solution is to say that a player may have a number of roles, and each of those roles can be represented by a different interface to a different underlying object. So a `Player` can be a `Batter`, a `Fielder`, and a `Catcher`, or any subset of the three (and, when we add an interface for `Pitcher`, a `Player` could be one of those as well).

It is a sad (but interesting) fact that no language, whether designed for programming a computer or evolved by some human culture, can describe the world in a completely natural fashion.‡ Those who have studied other (human) languages know that there are things that can be expressed easily in one that are difficult or impossible to express in another. Metaphor and poetry are, on some accounts, attempts to say the unsayable. Philosophers such as Kant, Hegel, and Heidegger push language to such extremes that it isn't clear what they are saying.

If human language can't capture the world, we certainly should not expect programming languages to do any better.§ Programming languages provide an abstraction of the computer that can be used to model things in the world, but there comes a point at which the expressiveness of the language is inadequate for the job of directly mapping the world and the language. When that happens, a good designer will recognize the mismatch, and make the trade-offs as best he can. Pushing the language beyond its expressive capabilities generally leads to bad design. You may be able to capture this part of the world in the dynamic structure of the program, but it won't look elegant in the language.

We will capture our relation between `Player` objects and the various statistic-gathering objects by using a form of delegation. We will extend our definition of the `Player` interface in such a way that we can obtain the various roles that such a player might have. To do this, we will add methods that will return an object supporting the appropriate interface for each of the roles. An example would look something like:

```
/**
 * Return a {@code Batter} object if this player has
 * any at-bats registered. Otherwise, return
 * {@code null}.
 */
Batter asBatter();

/**
 * Return a {@code Fielder} object representing the
 * Fielding statistics for this player, if the player
 * has any such statistics. Otherwise, return null.
 */
Fielder asFielder();
```

‡ What follows is another reflection of my early life as a philosopher, where I received a Ph.D. in the philosophy of language. Those who, like my wife, think that such study simply caused me to be interested in the uninteresting and the unintelligible should feel free to skip the next couple of paragraphs and start again with "we will capture this...."

§ If you skipped the last paragraph, you should skip this one, too. Start again at the next one.

```
/**
 * Return a {@code Catcher} object representing
 * the catching statistics of this player, if the
 * player is a catcher, otherwise return null.
 */
Catcher asCatcher();
```

We also need to decide how to indicate that a Player object does not fill one of these roles. One way would be to throw some exception on the methods just shown if the Player did not fill the requested role. This would indicate that not fulfilling one of these roles is very unusual and somehow wrong. But that's not the case with these roles; indeed, most Player objects will not fill the catcher role. So we will take the approach of saying that if a Player object does not fill a role, calling the get () method for that role on that Player object will return null. This is similar to the convention in C of returning a marked value to indicate an error, which we earlier railed against when we talked about exceptions. However, in this case it would be very hard to ignore the error (which is one of the problems with the C approach), and in fact the return of null does make sense semantically—after all, what this value tells us is that the player in question doesn't have any of these sorts of statistics.

It would also be nice to find out before making a call to one of these methods whether the Player was going to answer in the affirmative when asked if it filled a particular role. We will do this in a way that is similar to how we tell what position a player fills, by defining an enumeration for the possible roles and a pair of methods that will allow setting a role and querying whether a role is held by the Player. Unlike the position, however, a Player can have multiple roles, which will change how we implement this in a moment.

First, we will define the enumeration that sets out the statistical roles for a player. We will add this enumeration to our Player interface:

```
/**
 * The roles that can be played by a player. These
 * roles determine which statistics will be gathered
 * about the player.
 */
public enum Roles {
    Batter, Fielder, Catcher
}
```

Next, we add two methods to our interface, one that lets us add a role and another that lets us find out whether the Player has a role:

```
/**
 * Queries if the {@code Player} has the
 * indicated role. Returns {@code true} if the
 * player does have the role, and {@code false}
 * otherwise. Note that a player can have multiple
 * roles.
 * @param a role as defined in {@link Roles}
 * @return {@code true} if the player has the
```

```
 * role, and {@code false} otherwise.
 */
boolean hasRole(Roles role);

/**
 * Add a role to the set of roles for which
 * statistics are gathered by this player.
 * Adding a role multiple times has no effect
 * beyond the initial addition of the call. Roles
 * cannot be removed once assigned to a
 * player.
 * @param role the {@link Role} to be
 * added to the set of statistics for this
 * player.
 */
void addRole(Roles role);
```

Supporting these changes in our implementation is pretty straightforward. We will keep fields holding objects that support the Batter, Fielder, and Catcher interfaces. We will initialize these as null objects, but when the role is added, we will allocate the object and start keeping the statistics. There is a tricky bit in this because Catcher is a subtype of Fielder, but it's nothing that we can't handle. While we are at it, we will also put a method that returns a reference to the Player object in each of the Batter, Fielder, and Catcher interfaces, and add these methods to the corresponding implementation.

Of more interest to us here is how we keep track of the roles for a Player. We could keep a series of boolean fields, but that seems excessive. We could build our own bit string, but that would mean writing a lot of code.

Or we can look at the collections and see that there is a special Set that is made just for this kind of thing. This is the EnumSet, which gives us Set semantics over an enumeration. It is a parameterized collection, so we need to declare it as an EnumSet<Roles>, but doing that gives us exactly what we want. Making all these changes gives us a Player Impl class that looks like the following (eliding the methods that haven't changed):

```
package org.oreilly.javaGoodParts.examples.impl;

import java.io.FileInputStream;
import java.io.FileOutputStream;
import java.io.IOException;
import java.io.ObjectInputStream;
import java.io.ObjectOutputStream;
import java.io.Serializable;
import java.util.EnumSet;
import java.util.Random;
import org.oreilly.javaGoodParts.examples.statistics.Batter;
import org.oreilly.javaGoodParts.examples.statistics.Catcher;
import org.oreilly.javaGoodParts.examples.statistics.Fielder;
import org.oreilly.javaGoodParts.examples.statistics.Player;
import org.oreilly.javaGoodParts.examples.statistics.Team;
```

```java
/**
 *
 *
 */
public class PlayerImpl implements Player, Serializable {

    private static long serialVersionUID = 1;
    private int id;
    private String name;
    private Team team;
    private Position pos = Position.Utility;
    private EnumSet<Roles> roles;
    private boolean changed = false;

    private BatterImpl batterStats;
    private FielderImpl fielderStats;
    private CatcherImpl catcherStats;

    ...

    public boolean hasRole(Roles role){
        return roles.contains(role);
    }

    public void addRole(Roles role){
        if (roles.contains(role))
            return;
        switch (role){
            case Batter:
                batterStats = new BatterImpl();
                break;
            case Fielder:
                fielderStats = new FielderImpl();
                break;
            case Catcher:
                if (roles.contains(Roles.Fielder)){
                    catcherStats = new CatcherImpl(fielderStats);
                    fielderStats = catcherStats;
                } else {
                    catcherStats = new CatcherImpl();
                    roles.add(Roles.Fielder);
                }
                break;
        }
        roles.add(role);
    }

    public Batter asBatter(){
        return batterStats;
    }

    public Fielder asFielder(){
        return fielderStats;
    }
```

```
    public Catcher asCatcher(){
        return catcherStats;
    }
}
```

This implementation approach is not the only one we could take (although it does show the value of the `EnumSet`), and it does have its own problems. The `EnumSet roles` duplicates information that we already have (in a less direct way) in the `batterStats`, `fielderStats`, and `catcherStats` fields. Further, we now have two places where we have information that should be correlated. We could have complicated the implementation of the `hasRole()` method by determining the answer through examining the various `Stats` fields. Whether you prefer the more complex implementation or the field correlation is, to some extent, a matter of taste and style. Either can be right, and both can have their problems.

Now, we did all of that so we could start putting together the kinds of lists loved by those who keep these kinds of statistics. We would like, for example, to be able to produce a listing of all the members of a team sorted by their batting average. We have all the information that we need, now that we can get the roster of players on a team, find out which of those players are batters, and get their batting average. So we could dive in and start writing a sorting routine for batting averages, or for any of the other statistics that we would want to use to rank the various players.

Or we could take a look at the collection classes to see if there is anything there that can help us. And, what do you know, there is. In particular, there is an interface for a `SortedSet`, and a `TreeSet` class that implements this interface. The `SortedSet` will give us an `Iterator` that will present the members of the set in increasing order, and the `TreeSet` is an implementation of that interface that backs the set with a `Tree`. Even better, we can create the `TreeSet` specifying a `Comparitor` object, which will determine the order of the objects in the `SortedSet`. Given the kinds of comparison that statistics weenies[||] like to use, being able to specify various orders (batters by on-base percentage and batting average minus walks) sounds like just the ticket.

Let's start with the `Comparitor` object. The idea of a comparitor is to supply an implementation of an interface that contains two methods. The first, `compare()`, allows any two objects of the appropriate type to be compared; it will return a negative number if the first object is less than the second, a positive if the first number is greater than the second, and zero if the first has the same value as the second. The second method is `equals()`, which should return `true` if the two objects are equal and `false` if they are not.

This seems pretty simple, but there are some rules that must be followed. In particular, the usual rules of logic should apply. If *object1* is less than *object2*, which in turn is less than *object3*, then *object1* had better be less than *object3*. And if *object1* is equal to *object2* and *object2* is equal to *object3*, then *object1* had better be equal to *object3*. You

---

|| "Weenie," in this sense, is a technical term and should not be taken to convey a value judgment.

can write a comparitor in which these rules are not observed, but if you do, you will almost certainly get what you deserve. It's a really bad idea to mess with basic logic, so unless you are a trained professional logician, don't do it.

This is actually a special case of the more general problem that has been introduced in other, less fortunate languages by allowing operator overloading. Although it seems like a good idea to allow users to extend the notion of, say, the + operator to objects such as complex numbers or vectors, allowing this tempts the less disciplined to overload the operators in ways that violate the logic of the operator. So when overloading +, one should ensure that the usual rules of arithmetic apply, so that, say, a + b - b = a remains true. There are some experimental languages that have introduced mechanisms that enforce such a requirement, but without these mechanisms it is up to the programmer to ensure that the usual conventions are followed. Java doesn't have operator overloading, but it does have a user-defined equality operator (the equals() method), the comparitor, and the hashcode() method, all of which must be implemented in such a way as to retain the basic rules of those operations.

It's also best if the implementation of a comparitor gives a full ordering of the objects being compared. This means that any two objects are such that either they are equal, or one is greater than the other (and the other less than the one). For our case of a comparitor that deals with batting averages, this means that we need to add some code that will order players who have the same batting average. And since we want to order all of the players that get put into a set, we will also want our comparitor to deal with players who have no batting average, either because they don't have enough at-bats or because they aren't batters at all (those pesky American League pitchers).

So our comparitor will first look to see whether the Player has the role of a Batter. If not, or if the player does not have enough at-bats to have a valid average, then we will just set their batting average to zero. We will also break ties in the batting average by using the player's identifier. It would be more user-friendly to break ties using something that makes sense to the user, like the player's name, but the name is not guaranteed to be unique, so there is a small chance that two players with the same batting average could also have the same name. This might not be very likely, but we will be paranoid. Since the Id is guaranteed to be unique, it's a great way to make sure that the ordering induced by our comparitor is a full ordering. We will also use the Id to determine equality: two Player objects will be equal if they have the same Id. Having made these decisions, the comparitor looks like:

```
package org.oreilly.javaGoodParts.examples.impl;

import java.util.Comparator;
import org.oreilly.javaGoodParts.examples.statistics.NotEnoughAtBatsException;
import org.oreilly.javaGoodParts.examples.statistics.Player;

/**
 * A comparitor that will rank players depending on
 * their batting average. If both players have a
 * batting average, the one with the higher average
```

```
 * is compared as greater than the other. Players with
 * insufficient at bats or who don't bat at all are
 * dealt with as if their batting average is 0. If two
 * players have the same batting average, they will
 * be compared based on their player ids, which are
 * guaranteed to be unique.
 *
 * This comparison will give a well-ordering to any
 * collection of players, based on their batting average.
 * Ties are broken by using the Id field of the player, which
 * is also used to determine equality.
 */
public class BattingComparitor implements Comparator<Player>{

    @Override
    public int compare(Player o1, Player o2) {
        float o1A, o2A;
        int retVal;

        if (o1.getId() == o2.getId())
            return 0;
        if (o1.hasRole(Player.Roles.Batter)){
            try {
                o1A = o1.asBatter().getAverage();
            } catch (NotEnoughAtBatsException e){
                o1A = (float) 0.0;
            }
        } else
            o1A = 0.0f;

        if (o2.hasRole(Player.Roles.Batter)){
            try {
                o2A = o2.asBatter().getAverage();
            } catch (NotEnoughAtBatsException e){
                o2A = (float) 0.0;
            }
        } else
            o2A =  0.0f;

        if (o1A < o2A)
            retVal = -1;
        else if (o2A < o1A)
            retVal = 1;
        else if (o1.getId() < o2.getId())
            retVal = -1;
        else retVal = 1;

        return retVal;
    }

    public boolean equals(Player o1, Player o2){
        return (o1.getId()== o2.getId());
    }
}
```

Now that we have a comparitor that will rank `Players` by their batting average, we can create a method that will print out the players on a `Team` by their batting averages. We will create a `TreeSet` of players, ordered by our comparitor. We will then iterate over that set, and print out the players in the order given by the iterator. The whole method looks like:

```
public static void FormatBattingAvg(Team toFormat){
        TreeSet<Player> battingSort =
                new TreeSet<Player>(new BattingComparitor());

        battingSort.addAll(toFormat.getRoster());
        float avg = 0.0f;
        for (Player p : battingSort){
            System.out.print(p.getName() + "\t");
            if (p.hasRole(Roles.Batter)){
                try {
                    avg = p.asBatter().getAverage();
                } catch (NotEnoughAtBatsException e) {
                    avg = 0.0f;
                }
            }
            else
                avg = 0.0f;
            System.out.println(avg);
        }
    }
```

We start by creating a `TreeSort` object, `battingSort`, using our `BattingComparitor` object as the ordering function. We then add all of the members of the supplied `Team` in a single call. This is another instance of the collections library saving us from having to write code. Although it would be easy for us to iterate through the players on a team and add them one by one, all of the collections allow this kind of batch initialization from another collection, meaning we have less code to write, test, and optimize. We then print out the players in the order induced by the comparitor, printing out the average of those who either aren't batters or have no batting average as 0.

Unfortunately, this will print out the players in ascending order of batting average, which is probably not what we want. We could change our comparitor to make it reverse the usual notion of greater-than, so the players with the higher average are printed out first. But doing such a counterintuitive thing is also a way of introducing bugs ("Did I mean really greater, or reverse greater?"), so we will take a different tack. We will still order in the set using the obvious comparitor, but we will print out our set in reverse order. The `TreeSet` class lets us get the last member of the set (in our induced order), and since it is a set, we can remove elements at will. So to print in reverse order, we would need something like:

```
public static void FormatBADescending(Team toFormat){
        TreeSet<Player> battingSort =
                new TreeSet<Player>(new BattingComparitor());

        battingSort.addAll(toFormat.getRoster());
```

```
        float avg = 0.0f;
        for (Player p = battingSort.last();
                null != p;
                battingSort.remove(p)){
            if (!p.hasRole(Roles.Batter))
                return;
            try {
                avg = p.asBatter().getAverage();
                if (avg == 0.0)
                        return;
            } catch (NotEnoughAtBatsException e){
                return;
            }
            System.out.println(p.getName() + "\t"
                    + avg);
        }
    }
```

This will do what we want, printing out the members of a team in batting average order with the best average printed first.

Random Access

So far, all of the collection interfaces and classes have allowed us to iterate through the objects in our collection one at a time and do something to those objects. Although this is useful, there are times when we would like to just find a particular member of a collection and do something with it. We currently have sequential access to all of the objects in a collection, but it would be nice to have some mechanism for random access as well.

Suppose, for example, we would like to get the statistics for a particular player on a team. We could just step through the Set returned by the getRoster() method until we found the Player object in which we are interested. But while the Java collections mean that we don't have to implement all of the data structures we learned about in our programming classes, we still learned something of value in those classes. One thing we learned was that linear search like this is a bad way to implement random access. It wouldn't be terrible in this case (since rosters for baseball teams tend to be fairly small), but we know that there has to be a better way.

As always, we should start by deciding on the interface that we want to support for this kind of access. Since we want to find particular Player objects that are associated with a particular Team, we need to add something to the Team interface. We want a method that will return a Player object associated with a Team, given some identification of that Player. Since all Player objects have a unique identifier, finding Player objects by that identifier seems like an obvious addition to the interface. But since the unique identifiers are not very easy for humans to remember, it would also be nice to have a method that would return a Player object given something easier for people to understand, such as the name of the player. This would suggest adding two methods along the lines of:

```
Player getPlayer(UUID playerID);
Player getPlayer(String playerName);
```

The first of these is fine, but the second needs to be refined a bit. Recall that we introduced the player identifier because of the possibility that two players could have the same name. But if that is possible, it is also possible that two players on the same team could have the same name. So the second of these methods can't be guaranteed to return a single player given a name. Instead, we will allow the method that finds Player objects by name to return all of the Player objects associated with the name in a Set. Usually, the Set will have a single Player object in it (or no Player objects if there is no one by that name on the team), but if there are duplicate names on the same team, we can return both Player objects and let the caller figure out which one she really wanted.

With this in mind, we change our Team interface to allow finding Player objects by identifier or by name so that it looks like:

```
package org.oreilly.javaGoodParts.examples.statistics;

import java.util.Set;
import java.util.UUID;

/**
 * The {@code Team} interface, which defines the notion of a team for our
 * statistics package. A team is, at first incarnation, simply a collection of
 * players. All teams have a name.
 */
public interface Team {

    /**
     * Return a {@code String} that is the name of this team.
     */
    String getName();

    /**
     * Return the players that are on this team. The set returned is a set of
     * player objects.
     */
    Set<Player> getRoster();

    /**
     * Add a player to the team.
     */
    void addPlayer(Player toAdd);

    /**
     * Remove a player from the team.
     */
    void removePlayer(Player toRemove);

    /**
     * Return a list of players who are on this team who have the supplied name.
     * In general, the returned list will either be empty (which will be the
```

```
 * case if there are no players on the team with the name) or a singleton
 * list. However, if there are multiple players on the team with the same
 * name, it will be up to the caller to decide which of the players in the
 * list is wanted.
 *
 * @param name
 *              {@link String} containing the name of the player whose object
 *              is wanted
 * @return a {@link List} of {@link Player} objects whose names match the
 *              supplied {@link String}. If there are no players with a matching
 *              name, the list is empty
 */
Set<Player> getPlayer(String name);

/**
 * Return the player on the team with the indicated player id. If no player
 * has the supplied id, return {@code null}.
 *
 * @param playerId
 *              The {@link UUID} of the player whose record is desired
 * @return The {@link Player} object for the player with the indicated
 *              playerId, or {@code null} if there is no player on the team with
 *              that id.
 */
Player getPlayer(UUID playerId);
}
```

Now we need to implement the new `getPlayer()` methods. Rather than iterate through the `Set` of `Player` objects that we currently have in our `TeamImpl`, we will add a couple of new fields that are collections themselves. What we want are ways of mapping from keys to `Player` objects, where our keys will be either the ID of a `Player` or the name of the `Player`. This is the functionality that is provided by the `Map` interface in the collections, so we will want something that implements that interface. We will use the `Hash Map`.

The mapping from IDs to `Player` objects is straightforward, since we know that the ID is unique for each `Player` object. We simply declare a new member field that is a `HashMap` from `UUID` objects to `Player` objects. This does require that we specify two type parameters, but the resulting declaration looks something like:

```
private HashMap<UUID, Player> byIds;
```

Since names might not be unique, the declaration of the map from `String` objects to a `Set` of `Player` objects is slightly more complex, looking like:

```
private HashMap<String, Set<Player>> byName;
```

Implementing our new `getPlayer()` methods is easy with these maps in the `TeamImpl` objects; we just take the ID or name supplied and return whatever is in the corresponding `HashMap`. We do have to change the implementation of our `addPlayer()` and `removePlayer()` methods to update the new structures, but the only real complexity there is finding out whether there is a `Player` with the same name already in the byName map and, if so, adding to the existing Set rather than creating a new Set. The resulting implementation looks like:

```
package org.oreilly.javaGoodParts.examples.impl;

import java.util.HashMap;
import java.util.HashSet;
import java.util.List;
import java.util.Set;
import java.util.UUID;
import org.oreilly.javaGoodParts.examples.statistics.Player;
import org.oreilly.javaGoodParts.examples.statistics.Team;

/**
 * A fourth implementation of the Team interface, using a HashSet as the backing
 * store for the Players on the team, after the interface has been changed to
 * return a Set from the getPlayers() method. This iteration adds methods that
 * allow getting player records in a random access fashion. One method allows
 * getting a {@link List} of {@link Player} objects for a player from the name,
 * and the other allows getting a {@link Player} object from the player id. To
 * do this, we add two {@link HashMap} objects to the private fields.
 */
public class TeamImpl implements Team {

    private String name;
    private HashSet<Player> players = new HashSet<Player>();
    private HashMap<String, Set<Player>> byName =
        new HashMap<String, Set<Player>>();
    private HashMap<UUID, Player> byIds = new HashMap<UUID, Player>();

    /**
     * Create a TeamImpl object, with the name supplied.
     */
    public TeamImpl(String teamName) {
        name = teamName;
    }

    /**
     * Return a <code>String</code> that is the name of this team.
     */
    public String getName() {
        return name;
    }

    /**
     * Return a set of the players that are on this team.
     */
    public Set<Player> getRoster() {
        return new HashSet<Player>(players);
    }

    /**
     * Add a player to the team.
     */
    public void addPlayer(Player toAdd) {
```

```
        players.add(toAdd);
        if (byName.containsKey(toAdd.getName())) {
            byName.get(toAdd.getName()).add(toAdd);
        } else {
            HashSet<Player> newSet = new HashSet<Player>();
            newSet.add(toAdd);
            byName.put(toAdd.getName(), newSet);
        }
        byIds.put(toAdd.getId(), toAdd);
    }

    /**
     * Remove a player from the team.
     */
    public void removePlayer(Player toRemove) {
        players.remove(toRemove);
        byName.get(toRemove.getName()).remove(toRemove);
        if (byName.get(toRemove.getName()).isEmpty()) {
            byName.remove(toRemove.getName());
        }
        byIds.remove(toRemove.getId());
    }

    @Override
    public Set<Player> getPlayer(String name) {
        return byName.get(name);
    }

    @Override
    public Player getPlayer(UUID playerId) {
        return byIds.get(playerId);
    }
}
```

Once again, the joy of the Java environment is that we needed to write very little code to add this random access functionality to our Team objects. The collections classes that are already part of the platform did most of the heavy lifting for us.

Some Last Thoughts

This chapter has gone on quite long enough, and I hope that what has come so far has convinced you that the collections in Java are one of the good parts of the library. But before we go on to something else, I need to mention a couple of things.

The first can be seen if we look at the signature of a method we used in our last formatting examples, the addAll() method of TreeSet. Like all of the collections, TreeSet is generic, but this method is generic in a somewhat odd way, with a signature of:

```
boolean addAll(Collection<? extends E> c)
```

The argument declaration is something that we haven't discussed thus far: a wildcard parameter. This parameter says that the argument being fed into the `addAll()` method has to be a collection, and that collection must be made up of objects that have a type that extends the declared type used to parameterize the `TreeSet`. In our case, this means that the `TreeSet<Player>` that we declared can have sets of objects that extend the interface `<Player>` as well as objects that simply implement exactly that interface. This is because the subtyping relation that holds between classes does not transfer to collections of those classes. To get something like that requires extra syntax in the generics systems. I won't go into all of the possibilities here, but if you are going to implement a generic collection (as opposed to using such a collection), you will need to consult more advanced writings to understand how this works.

Finally, I should note the possible use of one of the more peculiar exception classes in the collections. This is the `java.lang.UnsupportedOperationException`, a runtime exception that was introduced specially for the collections classes.

The motive for introducing this exception had to do with a common problem when designing collection classes. There are all kinds of interrelationships between various kinds of collections that get used for specialized reasons. The obvious example is a standard `Set`, which allows you to add, remove, and query for objects, along with a read-only `Set` (that allows query, but no add or remove), the remove-only `Set` (that is created with some set of objects that can be queried or removed, but never has new objects added), and the add-only `Set` (objects can check in, but they can never check out).

Trying to model such variation in the type hierarchy of the collections can lead to a very messy type system, if it can work at all. You can end up with lots of interfaces that have only a single method, or class hierarchies that are deep and complex. Again, we run into the expressive limitations of the language and have to decide between our deep-seated sense of what is right and our engineering desire to do something that will work and can be understood.

Rather than try to reflect this variation in the type system, the original designers of the collections library decided that it would be better to introduce an exception that could be thrown by classes that are specialized in such a way that they don't implement all of the methods in their interface. So a read-only `Set`, on this theory, would still have an `add()` method. But the implementation of that method would throw an `UnsupportedOperationException`. Further, since programmers wouldn't want to have to declare this exception on every method that in the future might not be implemented in a collection class, and since programmers using the collections wouldn't want to be forced to guard against that exception (especially for those implementations that would never throw the exception, because they do implement all of the interface), the exception was made a runtime exception. It needs to be neither declared as part of a method signature nor caught by the caller of the method.

Which, of course, calls into question the notion of Java as a type-safe language. If you squint really hard, perhaps it is true that a read-only Set implements the add operation, but that implementation is done in a way that causes your program to fail with an uncaught exception.

Implementing methods by throwing this exception is, fortunately, not very common. In fact, the main use these days is in interactive development tools, which use this exception as a default implementation of methods in automatically generated code. But you should check the documentation for collections carefully to see whether the collection throws this exception for any part of the implementation. If they use it for an implementation without documentation, you should get a better collection implementation.

I will end this chapter with a simple observation. The collections in Java are useful additions to every programmer's toolkit. But they are also the reason for introducing generics (in the name of type safety) and the UnsupportedOperationException (in the name of simplicity). As long as neither one bites you, the irony is rather entertaining. It is also an indication that the Java environment is a complex creation resulting from the efforts of many people over a reasonably long period of time. When the UnsupportedOperationException was introduced, one set of designers made the decision that a flatter type hierarchy was preferable to strong typing. When generics and parameterized types were introduced (some number of years later), a (mostly) different set of designers made the decision that compiler type checking was vital. Being separated by time, the two groups couldn't have gotten together to make their decisions consistent. As we have seen before, history clarifies stupidity.

CHAPTER 9

Remote Method Invocation and Object Serialization

So far, I have talked a lot about how to build a program. But just as all programs can be broken down into more basic objects, most programs these days are part of a larger system of interacting programs. Breaking a system apart into a number of different programs has a lot of advantages, including independence of failure, security through isolation of parts, and the ability to change parts without interrupting the overall system. But it also requires that there be some way for the various programs to interact.

Historically, programs have interacted in different ways depending on how those programs were deployed. Programs that were guaranteed to run on the same computer would interact using inter-process communication mechanisms (IPCs), whereas programs that might be running on different computers would use some form of network communication. The communication might take a low-level form such as sockets, where the communicating programs send bits over the wire and are responsible for interpreting those bits. But since the early 1980s, a more common form of communication has been remote procedure call (RPC), which wraps much of the mechanism used to communicate between programs in a façade that makes the communication look like a procedure or method call.

Java's Remote Method Invocation (RMI) system is, on the surface, such a remote procedure call mechanism. Indeed, over the years, RMI has been expanded in a number of ways so that some uses (such as RMI over IIOP) are just a Java wrapper over more common RPC mechanisms (in the case of RMI over IIOP, the wrapper is around the CORBA RPC system).

But the original RMI* (now sometimes called RMI over JRMP) is a lot more interesting than it might first appear. It can also be very useful. Understanding what it can do and how to use it can make a programmer's life easier and more interesting. To fully understand RMI, we also need to dip into object serialization, which was originally used simply to pass arguments and return values in RMI, but is now used for much more. These two parts of Java are often maligned, misunderstood, and abused. But once understood, they are definitely in the good parts of Java.†

The Basics

So far we have built a system that lets us keep track of the statistics for baseball teams. But we haven't thought much about how the data for the statistics package gets entered into the system. We could just have a program that allows us to enter all of the statistics by hand from the keyboard. But the games are played all over the country, and it would be nice if we could let local observers enter statistics from wherever those statistics were gathered. This sounds like a fairly simple distributed system, where a central server is used to receive the statistics from clients somewhere out there on the network. Just the sort of thing that RMI was designed to do.

We start, as always, by defining the interface that the remote service will present to the outside world. Since we are assuming that the statistics will be sent after the game, we can have them all sent at once, so we start with a very simple interface that takes the bundle of statistics in a single call. For reasons that will become apparent when we talk about the way that we are going to hand back the game statistics, we also want to be able to get the roster for the teams that will be playing. We begin with an interface that has two methods that will be available from another address space, which looks like:

```
package org.oreilly.javaGoodParts.examples.statistics;

import java.rmi.Remote;
import java.rmi.RemoteException;
import java.util.Set;

/**
 * An interface for a simple server that can be
 * used to record the statistics for a game. The
```

---

* Remote Method Invocation has an interesting history. The original plan for distributed computing in Java made a Linda-like communication system the central mechanism for communication between virtual machines. Ann Wollrath, then working for Sun Labs, argued that an RPC system would be needed to implement such a system, and so was given the OK to work on an RPC layer that was not originally intended to become public. The resulting system was such a good fit into the Java programming environment that it became public in Java 1.1. The Linda-like communication system was produced as JavaSpaces, but never received the adoption of RMI.

† In the spirit of full disclosure, I should admit that I am not a disinterested observer of RMI. The original work for RMI was done in a group that I led (although I was working on other things at the time), and I've been associated with the team and the technology from early on in its life. So in some ways, writing about RMI is like writing about my children, with the main difference being that more people are interested in RMI.

```
 * server will take all of the statistics from a complete
 * game and enter them into the system.
 */
public interface StatRecorder extends Remote{
    /**
     * Record the statistics of a game. The statistics
     * are passed in as a {@link BoxScore} object.
     * @param stats a {@link BoxScore} containing
     * the batting and fielding statistics for the game
     * @throws RemoteException if there is
     * a problem with the underlying network or the
     * RMI system
     */
    void recordGame(BoxScore stats)
            throws RemoteException;

    /**
     * Return a list of the players on a team, where the
     * team is identified by name.
     * @param forTeam a {@link String} that is the name
     * of the team whose roster is desired
     * @return a {@link Set} of {@link Player} objects
     * that are the players on this team
     * @throws RemoteException if there is a problem
     * with the underlying network or the RMI system
     */
    Set<Player> getRoster(String forTeam)
            throws RemoteException;
}
```

There are two things to notice about this interface. The first is that the interface extends `java.rmi.Remote`. This is a marker interface, indicating that the interface that extends it will be used to define methods that will be made available to calls from other address spaces. We will look at how this happens when we look at the implementation of our interface. As a marker interface, it doesn't add any methods to the interface extending it.

The second thing to notice is that the two methods in the interface, `recordGame()` and `getRoster()`, are declared as throwing `java.rmi.RemoteException`. Any remotely accessible method in RMI needs to declare itself as throwing this exception (or a super-type of this exception). This is not an exception that will be thrown by the implementation of the server code, but rather an exception that will be thrown by the RMI runtime to indicate a problem with the network or with the internal workings of RMI. This exception reminds the programmer that the call being made is not a local call, but may in fact be subject to all of the failure modes of a networking call, including partial failure and long latency. It is up to the application to figure out how it wants to deal with such failures, but the fact that the exception is a user-level exception means that some thought has to be given to handling such failure. Any call to this method will need to be in a `try catch` block, with an exception handler supplied for the `RemoteException`.

The first method defined in this interface takes a single argument of type **BoxScore**. This argument is meant to be a shorthand way of encapsulating all of the relevant statistics for a game in a single object. Our definition of this interface is:

```
package org.oreilly.javaGoodParts.examples.statistics;

import java.util.List;
import java.util.UUID;

/**
 * An interface that will allow passing all of the statistics from a single game
 * to a {@link StatRecorder}, which will record the statistics for that game.
 */
public interface BoxScore {
    /**
     * Get a {@link List} of the names of the teams that played the game. There
     * should be exactly two teams in the List.
     *
     * @return A {@link List} of {@link String} that are the names containing
     *         the two teams that played the game
     */
    List<String> getTeams();

    /**
     * Get a {@link List} of the ids of the players who were in the game for the
     * indicated team.
     *
     * @param forTeam
     *              The {@link String} name of the team for which the list of
     *              players returned plays
     * @return a {@link List} of {@link UUID} identifying who played for the
     *         team in the game being reported
     */
    List<UUID> getPlayers(String forTeam);

    /**
     * Get the position played by the particular player today.
     *
     * @param forPlayer
     *              The {@link UUID} which is the player id of the player whose
     *              position for the game is being reported
     * @return the {@link Player.Position} played by the player in this game
     * @throws DidNotPlayException
     *               if the player did not play in the game being reported
     */
    Player.Position getPosition(UUID forPlayer) throws DidNotPlayException;

    /**
     * Gets a list of the at-bat results for a player.
     *
     * @param playerID
     *              the {@link UUID} for the player whose batting is being
     *              reported
```

```
     * @return a list of {@link Batter.AtBatResults} for the player in the
     *          particular game. If the player did not bat in the game, or if the
     *          player did not play in the game, the list will be empty
     * @throws DidNotPlayException
     *            if the player did not bat in the game being reported.
     */
    List<Batter.AtBatResult> getBatting(UUID playerID)
            throws DidNotPlayException;

    /**
     * Gets a list of the fielding results for the indicated player in this
     * game. Note that unlike the {@link #getPosition(UUID)} and
     * {@link #getBatting(UUID)} methods, this method will not throw a
     * {@link DidNotPlayException}, as a player may participate in a full game
     * and never make a defensive play.
     *
     * @param forPlayer
     *            the {@link UUID} player id for the player whose fielding
     *            results are being reported
     * @return a list of {@link Fielder.AttemptResult} for the player in the
     *          particular game. If the player made no plays in the field, or did
     *          not play, the list will be empty
     */
    List<Fielder.AttemptResult> getFielding(UUID forPlayer);

    /**
     * Gets the number of passed balls being reported for a particular player in
     * this game. Note that this should only be called if the player had the
     * {@link Player.Position} of catcher sometime during the game.
     *
     * @param forPlayer
     *            The {@link UUID} player id for the player whose passed ball
     *            count is being reported
     * @return the number of passed balls recorded for the player during the
     *          game. If there were no passed balls for the player, or if the
     *          player was not catching during the game, or if the player did not
     *          play, the returned value will be 0
     */
    int getPassedBalls(UUID forPlayer);
}
```

Note that in this interface, we are identifying teams by their names (since we pass
String objects back and forth) and identifying players by their player IDs, which are
UUID objects. We could just pass the Team and Player objects back and forth over the
network, but these are much larger than the String and UUID objects, and we are trying
to keep our communication overhead minimal. This means that the clients reporting
the scores need to find out the player IDs for all of the players on a team. This could
be done by having those UUID objects be well known in some way (published in a newspaper, for example). But a more self-contained mechanism is to allow the clients to get
a roster of the players on a team by talking with the StatRecorder server, which is the
purpose of our second method in the interface.

Implementing the BoxScore interface is reasonably easy, especially if we ignore the details of how the data would get into this object (which, for the sake of simplicity in this example, we will). A quick implementation would look something like:

```java
package org.oreilly.javaGoodParts.examples.impl;

import java.io.Serializable;
import java.util.Hashtable;
import java.util.LinkedList;
import java.util.List;
import java.util.UUID;
import org.oreilly.javaGoodParts.examples.statistics.Batter.AtBatResult;
import org.oreilly.javaGoodParts.examples.statistics.BoxScore;
import org.oreilly.javaGoodParts.examples.statistics.DidNotPlayException;
import org.oreilly.javaGoodParts.examples.statistics.Fielder.AttemptResult;
import org.oreilly.javaGoodParts.examples.statistics.Player.Position;

/**
 * An implementation of the {@link BoxScore} interface, ignoring
 * all of the little details like how the data that populates the private
 * fields is actually placed into the object.
 */
public class BoxScoreImpl implements BoxScore, Serializable {
    private static final long serialVersionUID = 1L;

    private LinkedList<String> teams
            = new LinkedList<String>();
    private Hashtable<String, List<UUID>> whoPlayed
            = new Hashtable<String, List<UUID>>();
    private Hashtable<UUID, Position> positions
            = new Hashtable<UUID, Position>();
    private Hashtable<UUID, List<AtBatResult>> atBats
            = new Hashtable<UUID, List<AtBatResult>>();
    private Hashtable<UUID, List<AttemptResult>> fielding
            = new Hashtable<UUID, List<AttemptResult>>();
    private Hashtable<UUID, Integer> passedBalls
            = new Hashtable<UUID, Integer>();

    public BoxScoreImpl(String team1, String team2){
        teams.add(team1);
        teams.add(team2);
    }
    @Override
    public List<String> getTeams() {
        return(teams);
    }

    @Override
    public List<UUID> getPlayers(String forTeam) {
        return(whoPlayed.get(forTeam));
    }

    @Override
    public Position getPosition(UUID forPlayer) throws DidNotPlayException {
        if (positions.contains(forPlayer))
```

```
                return positions.get(forPlayer);
            else
                throw new DidNotPlayException();
        }

        @Override
        public List<AtBatResult> getBatting(UUID playerID)
                throws DidNotPlayException {
            if (atBats.get(playerID) == null) {
                throw new DidNotPlayException();
            } else {
                return atBats.get(playerID);
            }
        }

        @Override
        public List<AttemptResult> getFielding(UUID forPlayer) {
            return fielding.get(forPlayer);
        }

        @Override
        public int getPassedBalls(UUID forPlayer) {
            return passedBalls.get(forPlayer).intValue();
        }

    }
```

The only really interesting thing here is that along with the interface BoxScore, the BoxScoreImpl class implements an additional interface, Serializable. This allows objects of this class to be passed from one address space to another via RMI. I will have a lot more to say about this in the next section; for now, just note that this object implements that second interface, which has no methods.

A simple implementation of the server will assume that it is run as part of a program that has already constructed all of the Team and Player objects, and can pass the Team objects into the server implementation. The code will look something like:

```
package org.oreilly.javaGoodParts.examples.impl;

import java.rmi.RemoteException;
import java.rmi.registry.LocateRegistry;
import java.rmi.registry.Registry;
import java.rmi.server.UnicastRemoteObject;
import java.util.Hashtable;
import java.util.List;
import java.util.Set;
import java.util.UUID;
import org.oreilly.javaGoodParts.examples.statistics.BoxScore;
import org.oreilly.javaGoodParts.examples.statistics.Player;
import org.oreilly.javaGoodParts.examples.statistics.StatRecorder;
import org.oreilly.javaGoodParts.examples.statistics.Team;
```

```
/**
 * An implementation of the StatRecorder interface. This will
 * create a server that is exported using the default RMI registry
 * (which will need to be started by some other means) on the
 * standard port (1099). The server will name itself Recorder,
 * and can be found by clients if they know the machine on which
 * the server is running.
 */
public class StatRecorderImpl implements StatRecorder {

    private Hashtable<String, Team> teams = new Hashtable<String, Team>();
    private Registry registry;
    private StatRecorder myStub;

    StatRecorderImpl(List<Team> initTeams) {
        for (Team t : initTeams) {
            teams.put(t.getName(), t);
        }
        try {
            exportRecorder();
        } catch (RemoteException e) {
            System.out.println("unable to export stat recorder");
            System.exit(1);
        }
    }

    @Override
    public void recordGame(BoxScore stats) throws RemoteException {
        for (String teamName : stats.getTeams()) {
            Team toUpdate = teams.get(teamName);
            processScore(toUpdate, stats);
        }
    }

    @Override
    public Set<Player> getRoster(String forTeam) throws RemoteException {
        return (teams.get(forTeam)).getRoster();
    }

    /**
     *  Export a stub object so that calls can be made from
     * another address space thorugh that object. This is done
     * by putting the stub in a {@link Registry}, which itself
     * is a remote object that others can use to find the stub
     * that in turn is used to call the remote objects of this
     * implementation.
     * @throws RemoteException
     */
    private void exportRecorder() throws RemoteException {
        if (System.getSecurityManager() == null){
            System.setSecurityManager(new SecurityManager());
        }
        registry = LocateRegistry.getRegistry();
        myStub = (StatRecorder) UnicastRemoteObject.exportObject(this, 5550);
        registry.rebind("Recorder", myStub);
```

```
        }

        /**
         * Process the box score for a particular team. This
         * implementation will go through the players (by their
         * id), and call {@link upDatePlayer} for each player
         * that was in the game.
         * @param forTeam the team whose players are being
         * updated
         * @param game the {@link BoxScore} object that
         * contains the record of the game
         */
        private void processScore(Team forTeam, BoxScore game) {
            List<UUID> players = game.getPlayers(forTeam.getName());
            for (UUID id : players) {
                Player toUpdate = forTeam.getPlayer(id);
                updatePlayer(toUpdate, game);
            }
        }

        /**
         * Update the statistics of a particular player, given
         * the boxscore of the game. The actual implementation
         * of this method is an exercise left to the reader...
         * @param toUpdate
         * @param game
         */
        private void updatePlayer(Player toUpdate, BoxScore game) {
        }
    }
```

This is a pretty straightforward implementation in most respects. Our constructor takes a list of the Team objects that we assume already exist, which can be used to populate a Hashtable that we are using to store the association of teams by their names. This list of Team objects will also let us get to all of the Player objects in which we might be interested. We have an implementation of the getRoster method that returns a Set of Player objects that are on a team, and an implementation of the methods needed to process the BoxScore reports of games that are sent in.

The only really interesting method in this implementation is the private method exportRecorder(). It is this method that connects the implementation with the runtime for RMI, and it is this connection that allows other programs running in other virtual machines (perhaps on other physical machines) to call our implementation. This is a very short method, but it is worth looking at in some detail.

The first two lines of the method simply make sure that there is a security manager running. Java security managers are a dark art (and are not included in this book, because of its title), but they do protect the virtual machine on which they are running in a number of ways. Because RMI makes use of the ability of the JVM to dynamically load code, and because you don't want to load code without the protection of a security manager, programs utilizing RMI should always be run with a security manager. We will talk more about this later, but adding lines like the first two in `exportRecorder()` ought to be a reflex for anyone using RMI.

The next line finds an instance of an RMI `Registry` object running on the local node. These registries are simple naming systems, allowing an RMI server to register itself under a name so that clients of the server can find it. Only objects on a (physical) machine can register with the registry on that machine,‡ but clients on other machines can look up values in registries on any machine they can find. This call assumes that some registry is running in the environment on which the server is going to run. The standard `rmiregistry` is shipped as part of the Java Development Kit.

There is nothing special about the RMI registry, other than that it is a well-known place where proxy objects can be stored and found. Any remotely accessible Java object could allow proxies to be registered and then hand those proxy objects out to others. The registry is a bootstrapping mechanism that is part of the standard Java platform, and therefore is known to be available. But others can be (and have been) written.

The next line is where most of the heavy lifting gets done. Here is where we export our server to the RMI runtime, using a call to `UnicastRemoteObject.export()`. In this call, we indicate which object we wish to export and the number of the port on which we want the object to receive calls (we also could have specified a port of `0`, in which case the RMI runtime would have picked a port for us). The RMI runtime will create a dynamic proxy object that knows how to contact that port, and the RMI runtime itself will listen on that port for network messages, forward calls to the remotely accessible methods, and return the values of those calls to the proxy object. The proxy object is returned from the export call. This proxy object is itself an instance of a class that implements both the `Serializable` interface and any other interface that extends `Remote` and is implemented by the implementation class. In this case, that would be the `StatRecorder` interface.

The idea is that we can ship a serialized form of the proxy object over the network, where it can be deserialized and act as a stand-in for our `StatRecorder` instance. The client that has received the proxy can make calls on that proxy that will be packaged up and sent over the network to our `StatRecorderImpl`. Responses will be shipped back to the proxy object that will return those responses to the client.

Finally, we register this proxy object with the local registry, using the name *Recorder* so that clients wanting to send game results can find it. These clients will need to know the name or network address of the machine on which the `StatRecorderImpl` is running, but if they are supplied with that name or address, they will be able to find the registry,

---

‡ Actually, the situation is somewhat more complex than this, since low-level virtual machines such as Xen or VMWare mimic multiple physical machines on a single server. But referring to these as virtual machines confuses these with the Java Virtual Machine. An RMI registry would only allow registration on the same Xen instance. But we have only two words (physical and virtual) for at least three different things (the actual hardware, the emulation in a Xen-style machine, and a Java virtual machine), so there are times when it gets confusing.

obtain the proxy for our `StatRecorderImpl`, and make the calls that will let them send in the information that we need to maintain our statistics.

The calls to the registry or the RMI runtime could fail for a number of reasons. The runtime might not be able to build a dynamic proxy from the information we have given, or the registry might not be running. In these cases, a `RemoteException` will be thrown by the RMI system. Rather than trying to recover from such a problem, we simply rethrow the exception from the `exportRecorder()` method. In our constructor, if such an exception is thrown, we simply give up on the construction of our `StatRecorderImpl`, print out an error message, and exit the program.

Accessing the server once it has been exported and registered is a matter of finding the machine on which the server is running, accessing the registry to get the proxy for the server, and then making calls on that proxy. To do this, we could write a class that will be in the client and looks something like:

```java
package org.oreilly.javaGoodParts.examples.impl;

import java.rmi.RemoteException;
import java.rmi.registry.LocateRegistry;
import java.rmi.registry.Registry;
import java.util.Set;
import org.oreilly.javaGoodParts.examples.statistics.BoxScore;
import org.oreilly.javaGoodParts.examples.statistics.Player;
import org.oreilly.javaGoodParts.examples.statistics.StatRecorder;

/**
 * A component to a client that can be used to report
 * the results of games to a {@link StatRecorder}. This
 * class will get the roster for a team from a given server,
 * and send a {@link BoxScore} to that server.
 */
public class StatReporterImpl {

    /**
     * Get a team roster from a {@link StatRecorder} running
     * on the indicated host. If no server is running on
     * the host, or if the host cannot be contacted, the
     * method will return null.
     * @param fromHost name of the host on which the
     * server is running
     * @param team the name of the team whose roster
     * is desired
     * @return a set of {@link Player} objects that
     * make up the roster of the team, or {@code null}
     * if there is a problem contacting the server
     */
    public Set<Player> getPlayers(String fromHost, String team) {
        try {
            StatRecorder recorder = getRecorder(fromHost);
            if (recorder != null) {
                return recorder.getRoster(team);
            } else {
```

```java
                return null;
            }
        } catch (RemoteException e) {
            System.out.println("Unable to find roster for team " + team);
            e.printStackTrace();
            return null;
        }
    }

    /**
     * Send the results of a game to a {@link StatRecorder}
     * running on the indicated host. If there is a problem
     * contacting the host, print an error message on the
     * console.
     * @param toHost name of the host on which the server
     * is running
     * @param score the {@link BoxScore} for the game
     * being reported
     */
    public void reportGame(String toHost, BoxScore score) {
        try {
            StatRecorder recorder = getRecorder(toHost);
            if (recorder != null) {
                recorder.recordGame(score);
            }
        } catch (Exception e) {
            System.out.println("Unable to report game");
            e.printStackTrace();
        }
    }

    /**
     * A private method that does the work of getting
     * a {@link Remote} reference to the {@link StatRecorder}.
     * If there is a problem with the communication, or if
     * no server is running, a {@code null} will be returned.
     * @param fromHost name of the host on which the
     * {@link StatRecorder} is running
     * @return a remote reference to the {@link StatRecorder},
     * or {@code null} if there is no such server or if it cannot
     * be contacted.
     */
    private StatRecorder getRecorder(String fromHost) {
        if (System.getSecurityManager() == null) {
            System.setSecurityManager(new SecurityManager());
        }
        try {
            Registry useRegistry = LocateRegistry.getRegistry(fromHost);
            return ((StatRecorder) useRegistry.lookup("Recorder"));
        } catch (Exception e) {
            System.out.println("Unable to find StatRecorder");
            e.printStackTrace();
            return null;
        }
```

```
            }
    }
```

The two public methods in this class allow us to find the roster for any team from a remote server and send a `BoxScore` object to a remote server to report the results of a game. These methods look just like regular Java code, in which we call methods and handle the exceptions that might be thrown by those methods. That is the idea behind all remote procedure call systems—to make a remote call look as much as possible like a local call, while still making it clear that they are different. We know that these calls aren't really local, since they might fail because of network problems. That's why in our implementation of the `StatReporterImpl` we have to handle the `RemoteException` that both methods are declared as possibly throwing. Our handling of the exception is not all that sophisticated; we might have chosen to have our `getRecord()` and `reportGame()` methods also throw `RemoteException` to their callers, pushing the handling of the exception to a higher level in the code.

Binding to the `StatRecorder` server is handled by the private `getRecorder()` method. This method takes a string as an argument, which should be the network name of the host on which the `StatRecorder` has registered. Note that with the current default implementation of the RMI registry, this will also be the host on which the `StatRecorder` server itself is running, as only objects running on a particular host are allowed to add entries to the registry on that host. The first thing this method does is make sure that there is a security manager running in the JVM; because we need to download the proxy object for the `StatRecorder` server, a security manager must be running. The method then tries to locate the RMI registry running on the default port (1099) of the named host. If that registry is found, we then look up the `StatRecorder` server using the name `Recorder` (which we knew in advance). If such a server is running, this method will return the proxy object that is returned by the `lookup()` call. If there is a problem—either because of the network, a registry not being found, or no server registered under that name—an error message is sent to the console and `null` is returned.

There are a number of agreements that the client and the server in this system need to make as part of their configuration. The client needs to know the name of the machine on which the server is going to run and the port for the registry on that machine that corresponds to the registry that the server is going to use. The client also needs to know the name under which the server is going to register. These agreements are not specific to RMI; they are part of bootstrapping any distributed system. There are ways of minimizing these agreements (such as UP&P, Jini, or various web service systems), but the same set of problems needs to be solved.

We also have not supplied a very good way of handing the exceptions that might happen in our system. We could, for example, deal with the `RemoteException` thrown when trying to register our `StatRecorder` server by creating a new registry in which we could then export our proxy object. Likewise, on receiving a `RemoteException` in the client, we might try some other host or some other port to find a registry that contains a server named `Recorder`. How we deal with such exceptions will depend very much on our application, and will have a large impact on how failure-resistant our application is going to be.

Often, the problems that cause a `RemoteException` to be thrown have nothing to do with the way a program is written, and everything to do with the environment in which the program is run. RMI is really a part of Java that lets you build systems of programs rather than just a single program, so the environment in which that system is running is often the cause of hard-to-diagnose problems. For example, our approach to exporting our server assumes that the RMI registry is running on the default port. If there is no registry running when we construct our `StatRecorderImpl()`, or if there is a registry running on a different port, we will get a remote exception, and on looking at the stack trace, will see that the exception was thrown because the connection to the registry was refused. In fact, there was no registry there to accept the connection.

A more common, and often more frustrating, cause of a `RemoteException` being thrown has to do with a class-loading failure on the part of the registry. But understanding that failure and how to avoid it requires that we first learn some of the mechanisms that form the support for RMI. We will start with the way RMI sends objects, both parameters and return values, from one virtual machine to another.

Object Serialization

In order to send parameters to a remote implementation of a method and receive the results of a call to such a method, we need to be able to send the parameters and the return values over the network. For primitive data types this is straightforward,[§] only requiring that the sending JVM and the receiving JVM interpret the bits that represent the primitives in the same way. For objects, the case is somewhat more complex. The data in the object may be, at base, made out of primitive object types. But the object is more than just the data held by the object and the order in which that data is presented. An object includes an interface and the methods that allow one to use the interface to manipulate the underlying data. Objects can also contain references other objects. Getting all of this in some representation that can be sent over the wire, and reconstructing that representation when it gets to the other side, is the job of object serialization.[||]

[§] Well, it is now. In the early days of RPC systems, how to determine the byte order of primitives was a subject of considerable debate. So there has been some progress in computer science.

[||] What to call the process of converting an object into a stream of bytes that can later (and perhaps elsewhere) be used to reconstruct a copy of the object was, at one time, a subject of some dispute. One of the common ways to refer to the process was by using the terms *pickling* and *unpickling*. Prototype versions of the Java process followed this naming convention, but this was objected to by some members of the Java team (the passive voice is used to protect all involved). After considerable discussion, the terms *object serialization* and *deserialization* were agreed upon.

At the most abstract level, the object serialization system simply converts a Java object into a linear string of bits that can be sent over the wire (an operation known, confusingly, as serialization), and converts a well-formed stream of bits into a Java object (an operation known as deserialization). More accurately, object serialization will convert a graph of objects, rooted in some particular object, into such a stream and convert a stream into a copy of an equivalent graph of objects. This means that if an object being serialized refers to some other object, that referred-to object will also be serialized, and a copy of the object will be reconstructed when the object that refers to it is reconstructed. Object serialization will also annotate the stream of bits with the information needed to determine the class of the objects that are to be reconstructed, so that the code for the class can be associated with the data.

To see how this works, let's go back and take a look at our remotely accessible server, the `StatRecorderImpl`. This class implements the two methods of the `StatRecorder` interface, which itself is declared as a `Remote`, which allows the methods in that interface to be called from another address space. One of these, `getRoster()`, takes a `String` that identifies a team and returns a `List<Player>`, that is, something that is a list of `Player` objects. What the implementation in `StatRecorderImpl` actually hands back is in fact a `LinkedList` of objects, each of which implements the `Player` interface. In fact, these objects are themselves `PlayerImpl` objects. This is what you would expect in an object-oriented language. There are no simple `List` objects (since `List` is an interface) just as there are no `Player` objects (also an interface). The method tells us that what we will get back from the call to `getRoster()` is something that is at least a `List` and that the contents of the `List` will be at least of type `Player`.

But what does our client, the `StatRecorderImpl`, get when it makes a successful call to the `getRoster()` method? Not surprisingly, it gets just what the `StatRecorderImpl` sends, which is a `LinkedList` of `PlayerImpl` objects. What may be surprising is what is required for that simple answer to be the case. Getting a `LinkedList` is easy, as the `LinkedList` class is part of the Java platform, and therefore is available on any machine running a compliant Java runtime. But making sure that the `PlayerImpl` object can be made available to the `StatRecorderImpl` is somewhat more interesting. RMI could simply require that all of the types used by clients and servers be present (and the same) on all machines running those clients and servers. But this requires a form of coordination that is difficult to scale. Instead, RMI uses object serialization to ensure that what you send is what you get.

To see how this works, let's look at how our `PlayerImpl` objects are sent from one virtual machine to another. Our `PlayerImpl` class, it will be recalled, was declared as:

```
public class PlayerImpl implements Player, Serializable {
```

We declared this as `Serializable` so that `PlayerImpl` objects could be written to a file by the `writeObject()` method of an `ObjectOutputStream`. While the `writeObject()` method is specified as taking an `Object` parameter, the documentation tells us that the method will throw a `NotSerializableException` if the method tries to write something that is not `Serializable`. Note that `NotSerializableException` is an extension of `IOException`, which is already declared as a possible exception generated from `writeObject()`. So it does not have to be declared as an additional part of the signature of the method, and the code catching the `IOException` will also catch the `NotSerializableException`. If you want to handle the `NotSerializableException` separately, you can do so (but be sure that you catch that exception before catching the `IOException`), but you won't be required to do so by the compiler. This is probably a design flaw, but there is nothing we can do about it now, other than make sure that our code will catch this.

Making a class of objects serializable is generally as simple as declaring the class to implement the interface `java.io.Serializable`. This is a marker interface, like `Remote`, so there are no methods that have to be implemented in a class that implements this interface. Instead, saying that a class implements `Serializable` simply indicates that the automatic object serialization mechanism can be applied to that object.

When object serialization was first designed as part of RMI, all Java objects were going to be `Serializable` by default. However, it was decided that this was a bad idea for a couple of reasons. The first was that it violated notions of security in the Java platform; when an object was serialized, its internal state could be observed (and, perhaps altered) outside of the usual security context of the Java Virtual Machine. Perhaps as important was the realization that declaring an object to be `Serializable` while not requiring that any methods be implemented did require the programmer creating the class to reflect on what that declaration entails.

One such implication is relevant from the start. If a class is marked as `Serializable`, the programmer constructing the class needs to ensure that either all parts of the object are themselves `Serializable` or are marked as excluded from the serialized state of the object. When we first made our `PlayerImpl` class implement `Serializable` back in Chapter 5, the fields of the class contained all primitive types or were of type `String`, which is itself `Serializable`. But when we added the various roles to the class in Chapter 8, we added fields that refer to classes that are not themselves `Serializable`. At the moment, none of the classes `BatterImpl`, `FielderImpl`, or `CatcherImpl` is `Serializable`. As things stand, any attempt to serialize a `PlayerImpl` object will throw a `NotSerializableException`.

We can deal with this in one of two ways. The first is useful when you are dealing with parts of an object's state that make sense only within the context of a particular virtual machine. For example, it is often convenient to store a file handle within the state of an object. But file handles are relative to a particular run of a program on a particular virtual machine; reconstructing the file handle in some other virtual machine doesn't really make sense and will result in trouble. For such fields, you can mark the field using the Java keyword `transient`, which will tell the object serialization system that the field should not be part of the serialized state of the object. Of course, when such an object is deserialized, it is up to the class to fill in some default value for the field.

But this is not the case with our `BatterImpl`, `FielderImpl`, and `CatcherImpl` objects. Each object contains information that will make sense if copied to a different machine (or copied to the same machine at some other time), so we would like these to be part of the serialized state of the `PlayerImpl` object. That means we need to mark each of these classes as `Serializable` as well. This is pretty simple; all we need to do is add `java.io.Serializable` to the list of interfaces each of these classes implements. When we do that, we should also make sure that all of the fields of these newly `Serializable` classes are themselves `Serializable`, and if not, we continue the process. Lather, rinse, repeat.

Well, almost. The perceptive reader will notice that we also add a `private static final long` field called `serialVersionUID` to each of these classes. The `serialVersionUID` is a remnant of an early attempt to deal with the versioning problem with Java classes. It is still useful in detecting version differences in classes, but the story of the `serialVersionUID` is a cautionary tale that may be of use to tell.

Object serialization allows us to take an object and convert it into a form that can be used to reconstruct a copy of that object, either at a different place (when it is used, for example, in RMI) or at a different time (when it is used, for example, in an `ObjectOutputStream`). But any time that you try to reconstruct a copy of an object at a different place or time, you face the problem of what to do if the class of the object has changed. Remember that objects are not just a collection of data, but are also the code that allows manipulation of that data. Since we aren't storing the code along with the object state in the serialized form, there is always the chance that when we reconstruct the object, the class that defined the data or the methods that manipulated the data have changed.

Java itself is defined as a name-equivalence language. This means that if two entities in the language have the same name, then those two things are the same within the Java framework. This is especially true for classes, which is why it is important to use packages (to assure that you have a different fully qualified name for your different classes). But being programmers, we# knew when object serialization was being designed that there might be cases where the same name in two different VMs identifies a class that had changed over time (or space), and that this could lead to very ugly problems.

The original idea was to introduce the `serialVersionUID` as a mechanism to allow the system to compare the class of an object that had been serialized with the class of that name available to the JVM in which the object was being deserialized. What the system did (and still does if you don't shortcircuit it) was compare a fingerprint of the class in the deserializing VM with a fingerprint of the class from the original context of the

---

#I have tried to write this without using the pronoun we a number of times, and it just doesn't work. Object serialization was first developed by Roger Riggs and Krishna Bharat while they were in Sun Labs, in the same group as Ann Wollrath (who at the time was developing RMI). I was the technical lead of the group, and we all discussed the work that was going on. So in this case, when I say we, those are the people who I mean, along with Ken Arnold, also part of the group, who was writing a book at the time.

serialized object, using a form of structural equivalence. In effect, the system wanted to make sure that all of the methods (including name, parameters, and return values) and all of the fields that defined the two classes were the same. The `serialVersionUID` was that fingerprint. Such a comparison shouldn't consider a change in order to make a difference, so it determined the `serialVersionUID` by taking a canonical ordering of the fields and methods and then taking a secure hash of those strings. This gave a single value that the system could use to determine changes over time in classes that were named the same. Attempting to deserialize an object that has a different `serialVersionUID` than the class with the same name in the deserializing process will result in an `InvalidClassException`, which is also a subclass of `IOException` and therefore not an explicit part of the signature of methods that deserialize objects.

This approach was well-intentioned, clever, and ultimately doomed. It worked as long as there were no Java compilers that would do clever things to the names of class members. It worked before there were inner classes, or enumerations, or a number of other features in the language that made the names of the methods and members vary from compiler to compiler.

The problem now is that if you let the Java runtime generate your `serialVersionUID`, the system will detect differences that aren't really there. This is the right failure mode, as it means that things will not be deserialized rather than being deserialized incorrectly. But you will still get an error that can't be explained by looking at the code, which is always something of a puzzle.

So you are much better off taking charge of the `serialVersionUID` yourself. If you assign it, you are also taking on the responsibility of changing it if you change the contents of your class. And this will only get you started on the very hard problem of trying to deal with different versions of classes as things change over time. But it will help.

It is important to realize that object serialization creates a copy of the graph of objects rooted at the object being serialized. It will do the best job it can of recreating that graph, keeping track of objects that have been put into the stream and putting references to that object only if the same object appears again. But object serialization can't perform miracles. If you separately serialize two objects, each of which references a common third object, when you deserialize the original two objects, you will get two copies of the object formerly referenced by both. Object serialization can't know what you are going to do in the future, and doesn't keep track of what you have done in the past (beyond the current graph of objects being serialized or deserialized).

One other thing to keep in mind concerning object serialization has to do with the way it treats static members of your class. These members are really part of the class of an object rather than the object, and so it doesn't seem to make sense to send them to a different address space as part of the serialize/deserialize operation. So all static members are implicitly treated as transient by serialization.

There is a lot more that can be done with object serialization, including writing your own custom mechanisms for a class by using the methods `readResolve()` and `writeReplace()`. But such specialized techniques are beyond the scope of this book. Further, they are not the kind of thing that makes object serialization one of the good parts of Java. What really earns the system entry into that group of features is the way it ties the portable code of Java into a system that allows you to transport objects, with their code, over space and time.

Subtypes in RPC Systems

Object serialization looks a lot like the marshalling and unmarshalling of objects that you will find in any remote procedure call system. What makes object serialization somewhat unique and what makes RMI very different from previous RPC systems is that the serial stream includes the information needed to identify and, when properly configured, find the code that goes along with the serialized object. This is not a big win when object serialization is used to write an object to persistent store and read that object back sometime later. But when combined with the Java Virtual Machine, this ability makes RMI unlike any other RPC system.

To see this difference, consider the issue of how to pass arguments and return values in an RPC system. The idea of such systems is that the arguments can be passed to the remote procedure, and the return values can be returned to the calling procedure. But in an object-oriented system, one of the basic patterns in method calls is to pass or return subtypes of the declared type into a method, and to utilize the particular implementation of some method in that subtype to perform the overall method, passing back something that is at least the type of the declared return type but perhaps something more. Making this work in an RPC system can be, in the least, somewhat challenging. But since RMI is designed to be used between JVMs, the system can use object serialization to get just this kind of behavior.

Consider a fairly standard form of RPC system such as the one that implements the Object Management Group's Common Object Request Broker Architecture (OMG CORBA) RPC mechanism. CORBA was meant to be a language-independent RPC system, so interfaces are defined in a special Interface Definition Language (IDL) that was originally based on a declarative subset of C++. The idea was that these interfaces could be used to generate stubs (that would marshal the input parameters, make a call to the remote procedure, and unmarshall the return value of the call) and the skeletons (that would unmarshall the input parameters, call the local procedure implementation, and return the results to the caller) in the target languages of the caller and procedure called. But since the system was programming-language-independent, all that could be passed were primitive types that could be mapped to all of the target languages, references to remote objects, and structures made up of those primitive types and references.

Thus, the only real objects that could be passed in CORBA were really references to remote objects. Although you could pass a reference to a remote object that was a subtype of the declared object type, when that object was unmarshalled (either as a parameter or a return value) the object created would be of exactly the declared type in the interface definition. In other words, the CORBA system would truncate the actual type of a (remote) object to the declared type of the interface. Given the language-independent nature of CORBA, and the variety of binary formats with which the system needed to interact, this was really the only reasonable approach. But it does mean that calling any parameter object in the remote procedure would result in another remote call (back to the remote object that was referenced by the passed-in object reference).

This means that if we tried our example in a CORBA system, either the List being passed back from the getRoster() method would have to be changed to a supported primitive data type (like an array) or what would be passed to our client would be a proxy to a remote object implementation of a list. Passing a proxy would keep the programming model the same (if we ignore the additional failure semantics introduced by RemoteException), but it would mean that any traversal of the list would involve a remote method call to get each Player object, with the subsequent performance implications. Further, what would be returned from such a list traversal would have to be a proxy for a remote implementation of a Player object, so any call to that object (for example, to get the player ID) would also be a remote call.

This is not a criticism of the CORBA style of RPC call. Given the language-independent nature of the CORBA system, this is the sort of thing that is required. Further, the whole goal of the CORBA system was to allow easy access to remote objects, not passing copies of language-level objects. CORBA does what it set out to do very well. But what it set out to do means that the kind of programming allowed by RMI is simply not possible.

A system much closer to RMI was the Module-3 Network Objects[*] system. Network Objects started as a language-based RPC system. Because it assumed that both the caller and the called were written in Modula-3, it could assume that the two ends of the RPC shared a single type system. This by itself is a powerful assumption, in that it allows the system to determine when two classes are the same or somehow related.

The Network Objects system also allowed objects to be passed by value as well as by reference. Like the CORBA system, Network Objects would allow a proxy for a remote object to be passed to some other address space. When a method on that object was called, the proxy would send the method request, along with the parameters, to the remote object, and receive and hand back any results of the call. But you could also pass an object from one address space to another, resulting in a copy of that object being recreated in the second address space. When that happened, any call to the object would not cause a remote call to be made, but would be processed locally. Like any other form of call by value, changes made in the copy of the object in the new address space would not be propagated to the original object.

---

[*] See Andrew Birrell et al., *Network Objects*, *http://birrell.org/andrew/papers/115-NetworkObjects-SOSP.pdf*. Note that two of the authors of the Network Objects system were also the authors of the first RPC system, on which much of the original CORBA RPC system was based.

The hard problem in a RPC system that allows passing objects by value is what to do when the object that is passed (either as a parameter or as a return value) is a subtype of the type that the method declares. If we go back to our `getRoster()` method of the `StatRecorder` class, we can see this problem in the return value of `List<Player>`. What is actually returned will be a copy of the objects that reside in the `StatRecorder` address space. But the actual type of the overall list will be a subtype of `List` (if it comes from an instance of our `StatRecorderImpl` class, it will be a `LinkedList`), and the objects stored in the list will be a subtype of the type `Player` (again, if it comes from an instance of our `StatRecorderImpl` class, it will be a `PlayerImpl`). How do we make sure that the correct classes are used to reconstruct the copy? For that matter, what is the right class to use?

The Network Objects system was built at a time when good performance required your code to be compiled into machine-specific binaries. Because of this, when an object was passed by value from one address space to another, there was no guarantee that all of the classes available on the sending machine were available on the receiving machine. Although the data could be sent from one machine to another, reconstructing an object requires not just the state but the code that is used to manipulate that state. The solution taken by the authors of the Networks Objects system was dependent on the fact that the Modula-3 language had only a single inheritance type system. So when an object was passed by value, it was reconstructed as the closest possible type residing on the receiving machine. If the actual type was available, the object would be reconstructed to its actual type. But if the actual type was not available, the reconstruction would walk up the type tree (which would be a line) until it found the first class that was resident on the local machine, and reconstruct the object as an instance of that type.

This approach was the best that could be done given the requirements of the system, but did lead to some complicating outcomes. The worst of these is that when passing an object by value you could never know exactly how that object would be reconstructed by the receiver unless you knew the classes that were installed on the receiver. This wasn't a problem for system classes, which could be assumed to be available everywhere. But for user-defined objects, this meant that you could not be assured that you would get the same answer to otherwise identical calls to different machines.

Like Network Objects, RMI was designed to be an RPC system that assumed both ends of the RPC call were written in Java.[†] And like Network Objects, RMI was designed to allow passing objects by value as well as by reference from one address space to another. Unlike Network Objects, however, Java compiles to bytecodes that can be run on any Java virtual machine, and the JVM allows classes to be dynamically loaded. So RMI was able to solve the problem of passing subtypes by value in a different way.

---

† Actually, the assumption in RMI is that both the sender and the receiver are written in such a way that they have a binary made up of compliant Java bytecodes. At the time that RMI was first designed, this was the same as the assumption that both the sender and the receiver were written in Java, but as more and more languages compile to Java bytecodes, this is less and less true.

When RMI passes a subtype by value, what gets reconstructed on the receiving side is exactly the same type as the original object. The serialized stream that is sent from one address space to the other is annotated with the actual class of the original object and a location on the network from which the bytecodes for the implementation of that class can be found. When the object is being deserialized, object serialization will first look at the set of classes available locally to see whether the actual class of the object can be found, and if so will use that local class. But if the class is not on the local machine, the code for the class will be obtained (if possible) from the source indicated in the serialization stream, and it will be loaded into the receiving JVM and used to reconstruct the object.

To see how this works, let's go back to the getRoster() method of our StatRecorder interface. All that the StatReporterImpl instance knows about the return value of this method is that it is a List of Player objects. If this comes from our StatRecorderImpl, what is sent is a copy of a LinkedList of PlayerImpl objects. The serialized stream is annotated with both the actual class of the objects in the stream and a location from which code has been made available if needed. When the StatReporterImpl process deserializes the return value, it should have no trouble finding a LinkedList implementation, as this is part of the standard Java runtime. But if it does not have a Player Impl class, it can obtain the right code over the network at the location indicated in the serialized stream. This code will be loaded and used for the objects that are being reconstructed.

Ensuring that the needed implementation code can be downloaded when needed to pass objects by value in RMI requires some work on the actual configuration of the runtime system. This has little to do with the programming of an application using RMI, but everything to do with the running of such programs.

Just as the classpath determines where the Java virtual machine will look to dynamically load code during runtime, there is a system property that determines how the serialized stream produced will be annotated to tell a receiving process where to look for classes needed for deserializing that stream. This property, which has the name java.rmi.server.codebase, should be set to a URL that is accessible from the client and that is the root of a hierarchy of classes (or a *.jar* file) that contains the code that may need to be downloaded. For example, to ensure that our PlayerImpl class is available to clients, we could start the program that contains the StatRecorderImpl with the system property:

```
-Djava.rmi.server.codebase=http://statServer.com/codeserver/codedl.jar
```

assuming that we were running something that could serve files from a URL (such as a web server) on the machine statServer.com, and that in the directories for that web server was a directory codeserver that contained the *codedl.jar* file that in turn contained all of the classes that might need to be downloaded by a client of the StatServerImpl. It is good practice to create a *.jar* file that contains all (and only) the classes that you want to make accessible to clients as part of the configuration of an RMI server. A common convention with such *.jar* files is to give them a name that ends in *dl* (for download).

There are times that this mechanism can cause considerable confusion and complexity, especially for systems in which lots of different machines are passing lots of objects to each other.[‡] But for most simple client/server applications, and even most complex ones, the ability to pass by either reference or value, and the ability to download code to ensure that pass-by-value passes just what you expect makes Java RMI a unique form of RPC. You need to be careful (the ability to download code is the main reason that Java RMI should be run only when there is a security manager present), but the end result can change the way you build distributed systems.

Like object serialization, there is much more to RMI than we have the space to discuss here. The system has a form of distributed garbage collection and a mechanism that will activate servers on demand. There are different ways of exporting objects and different ways of starting up places to register a remote object so that clients of that object can find it. But the thing that really makes RMI different is its ability to move code and data in a network of cooperating Java programs. That makes the system unique, and makes the system a good part of Java.

[‡] Those interested in these problems can do no better than to read the Sun Labs technical report by Michael Warres, *Class Loading Issues in Java RMI and Jini Networking Technology*, *http://research.sun.com/techrep/2006/abstract-149.html*.

CHAPTER 10

Concurrency

There was a time, not all that long ago, when it was easy to improve the performance of your programs. You could take a look at what a program was doing using a profiler and study the inner loops of the code. You could write dozens of test cases, varying the load on the program, to see which optimization was working under what set of circumstances. You could handcraft clever data structures that would save cycles per call. If you were industrious and lucky, all of this work would take about 18 months, at which time the new generation of processors would become available and your program would suddenly run about twice as fast. Lather, rinse, repeat.

But this pattern has changed recently. Cranking up the clock (and therefore the speed) on a processor has become harder and harder to do. People are now worried about energy efficiency, which goes down as the clock goes up. The corollary to the energy problem is the heat problem; chips are getting harder and harder to cool as they go faster and faster. It has been some time since the raw speed of the CPU has seen a significant bump.

We are still seeing the effects of Moore's Law; CPU designers are still cramming more and more transistors on each piece of silicon. But rather than using those transistors to make the CPU faster, they have moved to producing multicore chips, in which multiple copies of the CPU share a chip. The idea is that if you have multiple programs running on a machine, you can run each program in its own core and get twice the overall performance.[*]

---

[*] We will follow the chip makers and ignore all of the other things that impact performance, such as memory bandwidth, network latency, and the like. In fact, the cost of getting data onto the chip through the I/O pins, it can be argued, is the largest single factor in overall performance, and little has been done to change that in the past many years. The main effect of making the CPU run faster, on this view, is to allow more cycles to be burned while the chip stalls waiting for the data. But I digress....

Now, instead of the chip being twice as fast every 18 months, the chips seem to be getting twice as many cores every 18 months. The chip jockeys can still claim that they are doubling performance every 18 months, but now they mean that they can run twice as many programs concurrently.

These extra cores don't do anything to automatically speed up your program. Your program will take just as long to run as it did on the previous generation of hardware. Unless, that is, you have written your program to take advantage of these extra cores. If your program has a high degree of concurrency, so that it can run on multiple cores at the same time, doubling the number of cores available to your program could double the speed of that program.† But you have to write the program differently than you would write a standard, sequential program. You need to write your program to take advantage of concurrency.

Concurrent programming has always been difficult, and has usually been left to the low-level system wizards who can then provide a sequential view of the world to the average programmer. Java, however, was originally intended to be used in systems where a high degree of concurrency was the only way to get acceptable performance. As such, it has language constructs that can be used to build reliable concurrent programs. By utilizing these constructs correctly, you can take advantage of new advances in chip design. Even if you don't write highly concurrent code yourself, you should try to write any classes that are designed to be reused so that they are safe when used with highly concurrent code, which requires some understanding of the Java concurrency constructs. That Java has such constructs is a good thing, especially given current hardware trends. But it takes great care and thought to use these constructs correctly. So I will end this discussion of the good parts of Java proper with a gentle introduction to concurrency in the Java environment.

If nothing else, you should be aware of just how hard it is to handle concurrency correctly. This will give you more reason not to write your own multithreaded classes, instead using those that have already been written, debugged, and optimized when you can. The Java collections have a set of concurrency-safe implementations, and you should always use those in favor of any you may write yourself. You should also make sure that you read the documentation for classes to find out whether they are safe in a multithreaded environment, and make sure that you don't use classes that aren't safe as though they were. Finally, you should make sure that your own documentation is clear about whether multithreaded code can safely use your implementations.

Enough with the warnings: back to looking at how to use multiple threads of control in your Java programs.

We've already seen one way in which you could do this. If you can break your larger program up into a set of separate, smaller programs that communicate with Remote Method Invocation, you could make use of multiple cores by running the different

---

† Subject, of course, to the stipulations in the previous footnote.

programs together. This assumes that you are actually getting parallelism when you do this rather than just running a single hardware thread through different Java virtual machines,‡ but sometimes this can work just fine.

A more powerful approach tries to achieve currency in a single Java Virtual Machine by using multiple threads in that VM. Threads, unlike processes, can share the same address space, so they are able to communicate and coordinate through accessing the same memory. This can make inter-thread communication much faster than what you can achieve using RMI. However, this also means that the two threads can interfere with each other by trying to do different things to the same place in memory at the same time. The trick in concurrent programming is setting up the right protections to ensure that the memory shared by the multiple threads does not introduce new and subtle bugs.

The Basics

We've already seen a situation where it might be nice to have multiple threads running. The kinds of cases you hear a lot about these days are when you have a lot of work that can be broken down into parallel computations, and you place each of the computations in a separate thread. We haven't done anything like that, but we have encountered a place where we are making calls that could take a (relatively) long time to complete. It would be nice if we could make those calls, do some other work while the calls were completing, and then come back to them when we had finished our other work to get the results.

We saw possible examples of this in Chapter 9. Calls that go across a network can take a lot of time (for a computer), and if we can find something else to do while those calls are being made, we can make better use of our computing resources. But using a remote procedure call mechanism means that the call across the network looks like a local method call, which in turn means that we need to wait for the call to complete before we can do something else. There are some who have argued that this shows a basic weakness in the RPC paradigm, and that this approach to distributed systems should be abandoned in favor of some sort of message-oriented system. I will not go into that debate here, other than to say that with the use of concurrent programming techniques, such arguments don't really hold water.§

---

‡ Like many other terms in computer science, "thread" can mean different things in different contexts. There are hardware threads, software threads, and complex relations between the two. I will not go into the admittedly important distinctions between these uses of the term; you can get into the kind of trouble talked about in this chapter using any form of threading and concurrency.

§ At least they don't hold water with respect to the impact on the performance of the program. There are other arguments, having to do with the ease of programming or ease of reading, that could (and almost certainly will) continue. But since those are matters of style and taste, they don't terminate, so I will not try to rehearse them here.

Waiting for an RPC call to complete can cost us a lot of performance unless we make the call in a separate thread. If we create a new thread to do the RMI call, we can let that thread wait for the answer while we have a different thread do something else. This sort of approach helps even if we are on a single-core processor, where only one thread is running at a time. While the RMI call is pending, the other thread can be scheduled and run.

The simplest way to do this is to create a class that extends the base system class `java.lang.Thread`. Such a class will inherit a `start()` method that will kick off a thread, running the `run()` method that is also inherited from the base `Thread` class.

To see how this works, let's go back to our `StatReporterImpl` class. One of the things that class does is call a remote `StatRecorder` object to get the rosters for a team. The `StatReporterImpl` object can then use the roster to get initial information, such as the player ID, for those players in a game that the `StatReporterImpl` object is going to report to the `StatRecorder`. In our original implementation, the `StatReporterImpl` object made a call to a `StatRecorder` object to get the roster for a team, waiting until the call finished to do anything else. This might be fine if both the objects are on a local network. But if there is a more complex network between them, this call might take some time.

A different approach would be to build a class within the `StatReporterImpl` object that can be used to make the remote calls in a separate thread while the `StatReporterImpl` object does something else. We will make this class extend the base class `Thread`, and do all the remote work that we had been doing in the `StatReporterImpl` object. The class looks something like:

```
/**
 * A private inner class that can be used to obtain the
 * roster of a team. This class can be started on its
 * own thread and left to do its work. When the results
 * are needed, you can find out if the work is done by
 * checking the results of {@link isDone}. Once the
 * remote calls have completed, the value of the team
 * roster can be obtained by calling {@link getRoster}. Failure
 * will be indicated by a value of {@code true} for {@link isDone}
 * and a value of {@code null} for {@code getRoster}.
 */
private class RosterRetriever extends Thread {
    private String fromHost = null;
    private String forTeam = null;
    private Set<Player> roster = null;
    private boolean done = false;

    RosterRetriever(String fromHost, String team) {
        this.fromHost = fromHost;
        forTeam = team;
    }

    @Override
    public void run(){
        try {
```

```
            Registry useRegistry = LocateRegistry.getRegistry(fromHost);
            StatRecorder recorder =
                    (StatRecorder) useRegistry.lookup("Recorder");
            roster = recorder.getRoster(forTeam);
            done = true;
        } catch (Exception e) {
            System.out.println("Unable to get roster for team " + forTeam);
            done = true;
        }
    }

    boolean isDone(){
        return done;
    }

    Set<Player> getRoster(){
        return roster;
    }
}
```

The idea behind the use of this class is that we will create a single object instance for each team and `StatRecorder` object-containing host that we want to query. The `run()` method of this object tries to contact the host that was supplied as part of the constructor to find a `StatRecorder` server. If one is found, the method will then attempt to get the roster for the `Team` whose name was given as part of the constructor. Once the method is finished, either successfully or when an exception has been thrown, the `boolean isDone` is set to `true` and the method finishes. Note that the `run()` method takes no parameters and returns nothing; all of the work of setup is accomplished before the method is called, and all of the results are stored as part of the object state. In this sense, a method like this is something like the completions found in other languages. But the real reason to have such an object is to allow it to be run concurrently with other things that our program might be doing.

We can then call `start()` on a `RosterRetriever` object, which will execute the `run()` method. The `start()` method will return as soon as the thread is started, and we can run in parallel with that thread in our main program. When we actually need the roster, we will first see whether the work is complete by calling `isDone()`. If the result we get back is `true`, we can then call `getRoster()`. If the result of this call is `null`, we know that something went wrong. But if we get a `Set` of `Player` objects back, we will have gotten the roster for the team in parallel with doing other things.

We can make `RosterRetriever` an inner class that is seen only in the scope of the `StatReporterImpl` object. This will ensure that only individual objects of the `StatReporterImpl` class will use this kind of object. To use a `RosterRetriever`, we could add a method to the `StatReporterImpl` that looks something like:

```
/**
 * Create and start a {@link RosterRetriever}. The created object
 * will be initialized with the name of a host and a team, and will
 * be started so that it can get the roster for that team from the
 * {@link StatReporter} running on that host (if there is one). This
```

```
 * method will start a separate thread for the retrieval, and will
 * return while that thread is running.
 * @param fromHost name of the host to contact looking for a
 * {@link StatRecorder} to obtain the roster
 * @param team Name of the team whose roster is desired
 * @return the {@link RosterRetriever} created
 */
private RosterRetriever startRosterLookup(String fromHost, String team) {
    RosterRetriever getter = new RosterRetriever(fromHost, team);
    getter.start();
    return getter;
}
```

This method will create a `RosterRetriever`, initializing the team and host names, and then start a thread that will perform the `run()` method of that class. It will return the `RosterRetriever` object that was created, which we will stash someplace (a `Hashtable` mapping team names to `RosterRetriever` objects associated with that team would be a good candidate), and then our code could go off and do other things while this new thread makes the remote calls to get the roster for the team.

When we actually want to find the roster for a team, we will use the `RosterRetriever` object that was started up with that team's name. Prior to trying to get the roster, we will call the `isDone()` method, which will tell us whether the task has completed. If that comes back `true`, we can then call the `getRoster()` method. If that returns a value of `null`, we know that something went wrong. If we really wanted to know, we could add an `Exception` field to our `RosterRetriever` and a method to return that `Exception` object. More likely we will get back the `List` of `Player` objects that is the roster for the team. Best of all, we didn't have to wait while we got the roster. Our program could continue doing something else while all that was going on in a separate thread.

We can also try to get an updated roster by creating a new `RosterRetriever` object for a particular team (and host) and, when we think an update might be needed, calling `start()` on that object. We can create a new `RosterRetriever` object and `start()` it any number of times; each time we do, a new thread object will be created, started, and the remote calls made.

We can get exactly the same results in a slightly different way that also gives us more flexibility in how we run our background gathering of rosters. If we make the `Roster Retriever` implement the interface `Runnable`, we can create threads that will run instances of the class. Changing the `RosterRetriever` class for this sort of approach is easy; all we have to do is change the class declaration from:

```
private class RosterRetriever extends Thread {
```

to:

```
private class RosterRetriever implements Runnable {
```

The `Runnable` interface requires the implementation of a single method, `run()`, which takes no arguments and returns void. Fortunately, we already have such a method, so we don't have to add anything. This isn't surprising, as the reason for the `Runnable` interface is to allow classes implementing that interface to be executed in separate threads.

We do need to change the way we start off the RosterRetriever object. Rather than just calling start(), which the class inherited from Thread when it was an extension of that class, we need to create a Thread object, handing a RosterRetriever object into the constructor for the Thread. We can then start() the Thread object. So our startRoster Lookup would now look like:

```
private RosterRetriever startRosterLookup(String fromHost, String team){
    RosterRetriever getter = new RosterRetriever(fromHost, team);
    Thread rrThread = new Thread(getter);
    rrThread.start();
    return getter;
}
```

This has the same result as our earlier implementation, but we can now do other things to control the thread use in our program. For example, rather than allocating a new thread every time we want to run a RosterRetriever, we could have a pool of threads and take a thread from that pool if one is available or wait until such a thread was returned to the pool before fetching a remote roster. This would allow us to limit the number of threads that are taken up in this kind of background task.

As a final example before moving on to a different subject, let's take a look at how we could set up the fetching of a team roster on a regular basis, so we could be sure of always having the most recent lineup. To do this, we could just change our run() method so that it is an infinite loop that would end with a wait() on completing each iteration. But this means that the thread that runs the RosterRetriever is around all the time, which wastes resources. A better way is to use a Timer object, which can be used to schedule any number of recurring tasks like this using a single thread.

To do this, we first have to change our RosterRetriever class to be a particular kind of Runnable, the TimerTask. Once again, this just requires a change in the declaration of the RosterRetriever class, since the all-important run() method is common to Thread, Runnable, and TimerTask objects. So now our RosterRetriever is declared as:

```
private class RosterRetriever extends TimerTask {
```

We also add a Timer to our local state in the StatReporterImpl, something like:

```
private Timer taskTimer = new Timer(true);
```

Now we can use the taskTimer to schedule recurring runs of our RosterRetriever objects. To schedule a task, we could use a method like:

```
void setRetrieverUpdate(long hours, RosterRetriever rr){
    long millis = TimeUnit.HOURS.convert(hours, TimeUnit.MILLISECONDS);
    taskTimer.schedule(rr, System.currentTimeMillis(), millis);
}
```

This method will take a RosterRetriever object and a number of hours indicating how often we want to get an update on that object. Each RosterRetriever will initially be run when added to the `taskTimer`, and then will run again every `hours` hours. Note that we have to convert the interval from hours to milliseconds, which are the units used throughout Java; this is made somewhat easier by using the `TimeUnit` conversion functions.

There are lots of other ways to get multiple threads running in a program, as well as ways of querying and manipulating those threads. This is just meant to give a flavor of what can be done. By generating lots of threads, you can have your programming doing lots of different things at the same time, thus making better use of the computing resources that are available to you. That all of these mechanisms (and more) are part of the core language and libraries is one of the good parts in Java.

But there is a price to pay for using multiple threads in your code. You have to be careful, and you have to think hard, to make sure that the work being done in one thread doesn't interfere with the work being done in another. So before we get too carried away with the concurrency capabilities in Java, we should take a look at the dark side of highly concurrent code.

Synchronizing

Running multiple threads is a great way to improve the performance of a program. But be aware that having multiple threads in a program is like sharing a room with your little brother. It makes for easy communication, and a lot can happen in the room, but it is really easy for those who share the room to mess it up because they are sharing too much.

The sharing problem with threads comes because there is no barrier between the data that the threads can access. Unlike multiple processes, which have no access to memory other than their own, multiple threads have complete access to anything that the other is doing. This is an advantage for communication, but it means that you have to be very careful that one thread does not change the values that another thread is working with, and that each thread sees a consistent view of the shared world, even when another is updating that world.

We can see this problem when we turn our attention to the `StatRecorderImpl` class. We have made this class accessible remotely, allowing programs running elsewhere to obtain rosters and report box scores to the instances of this class. Server objects like this are generally run with multiple threads, allowing lots of clients to attach to the server at any time and getting their requests serviced in parallel. But if we are going to hand out lists of `Player` objects and also update those objects when box scores are sent to us, we need to make sure that we aren't going to report inconsistent statistics about those players. RMI, by default, will spawn a new thread for every incoming request. So we need to take a look at our `StatRecorderImpl` to see where things could go wrong in the multithreaded world.

What we need to worry about is code that updates the state associated with the StatRecorderImpl object. Fortunately, there is only one method where this happens: the processScore() method, which takes a box score report and updates all of the player statistics for the players in that game. The implementation of this method is pretty simple:

```
/**
 * Process the box score for a particular team. This
 * implementation will go through the players (by their
 * id), and call {@link updatePlayer} for each player
 * that was in the game.
 * @param forTeam the team whose players are being
 * updated
 * @param game the {@link BoxScore} object that
 * contains the record of the game
 */
private void processScore(Team forTeam, BoxScore game) {
    List<UUID> players = game.getPlayers(forTeam.getName());
    for (UUID id : players) {
        Player toUpdate = forTeam.getPlayer(id);
        updatePlayer(toUpdate, game);
    }
}
```

The question we need to ask ourselves is what could go wrong during such an update. There are two cases we need to consider. The first is what could go wrong if such an update is called on two different threads, which could happen if two games played by the same team were being reported at the same time. The second is what could go wrong if one thread is responding to a call to getRoster() while we were in the middle of a processScore().

The answer to both of these will depend on what is done in updatePlayer(), which we left as an exercise to the reader in Chapter 9. Let's flesh this out a bit now. A reasonable approach to such an update method might look like:

```
/**
 * Update the statistics of a particular player, given
 * the boxscore of the game. The complete implementation
 * of this method is an exercise left to the reader...
 * @param toUpdate
 * @param game
 */
private void updatePlayer(Player toUpdate, BoxScore game) {
    List<Batter.AtBatResult> batting = game.getBatting(toUpdate.getId());
    if (!batting.isEmpty()){
        updateBatting(toUpdate, batting);
    }
    /* Need to add further clauses to update other statistics*/
}
/**
 * Update the batting statistics for a player for a particular game.
 * This method assumes that the player is associated with some batting
 * statistics (e.g., that there is a {@link Batter} object associated
```

```
 * with the player.)
 * @param batter Player whose batting statistics are to be updated
 * @param results a list of the batting results for a particular game
 */
private void updateBatting(Player batter, List<Batter.AtBatResult> results){
    Batter batStats = batter.asBatter();
    for (Batter.AtBatResult r : results){
        batStats.atBat(r);
    }
}
```

What could go wrong if two such updates were happening at the same time? This will depend on the implementation of the `atBat()` method. A straightforward approach to the `BatterImpl` class implements that method as:

```
public void atBat(AtBatResult what) {
    switch (what) {
        case strikeOut:
            break;
        case fieldOut:
            break;
        case base1:
            hits++;
            bases++;
            break;
        case base2:
            hits++;
            bases += 2;
            break;
        case base3:
            hits++;
            bases += 3;
        case base4:
            hits++;
            bases += 4;
        case sacrifice:
            sacrifices++;
            return;
        case walk:
            baseOnBalls++;
            return;
    }
    atBats++;
}
```

This method looks like it can survive being called by multiple threads at the same time. It is just incrementing some counters, so the order in which it is called by two different threads won't matter. Indeed, it doesn't matter if one thread increments the `hits` counter, then another thread increments that counter and the `atBats` counter, and then the first increments the `atBats` counter. Even though there is an interweaving of the instructions, the results are the same.

So we seem to be OK, except that we have made two assumptions that, if they are not true, will cause us trouble. The first assumption is that the implementation of the

Batter interface that we get when we call `asBatter()` on a `Player` object will in fact be a `BatterImpl`. We could check this (using a call to `instanceof()`), but that defeats the idea of using an interface as the return value of the call `asBatter()`. That idea is to allow alternate implementations of the interface. But if we are allowing alternate implementations, we can't decide on the safety of our system through inspection of one of the implementations, unless we have specified the concurrency behavior as part of the interface (which we have not).

The second assumption is somewhat subtler, but can lead to just as much trouble. Even if we have the implementation shown earlier, we have to assume that the increment operations are atomic if we are going to avoid worry about multithreading. That is, we have to assume that an operation like `atBats++` happens without interruption. But that is going to depend on how the virtual machine is implemented. All we know is that an operation like `atBats++` is equivalent to the series of operations:

```
temp = atBats;
temp = temp + 1;
atBats = temp;
```

To see why this is a problem in an environment with multiple threads, consider the schedule where thread 1 comes in, sets `temp` to the value in `atBats`, increments the value of `temp` by 1, and then is stopped for some reason. Thread 2 then executes the entire sequence, starting by setting the value of `temp` to the current value of `atBats`. Thread 1 then begins again, assigning the value of `temp` to `atBats`. The effect of this schedule is to increment `atBats` by 1. But the correct result is to increment it by 2.

This is the kind of bug that will drive a programmer crazy. It will appear only when the thread scheduling is just so. You will write tests that will pass. All of the QA tests for the program will pass. The program might run fine for a long time. But someday, just the right sequence of events will occur and your program will give the wrong answer. And it will drive you crazy trying to find out why.

Nor are things much better if we think about one thread doing the updating while another thread returns a list of the `Player` objects. Imagine what happens if the `Player` object returned is in the midst of being updated. If the counter for `hits` or number of `bases` has been incremented but the number of `atBats` has not, then the statistics returned for the particular player will be off. It won't be that the statistics will simply be out of date; they will be inconsistent. This is not as bad as the earlier problems relating to dueling updates, as it will not corrupt the data, only return inconsistent data that will later be consistent. But for a package that is supposed to deal with such statistics, this is still not a happy result.

The way to deal with these problems is to use the `synchronized` keyword, which will place a lock on either a method or an object to ensure that only one thread will have access to the thing locked at any time. This gives us the tool that we need to make our code safe, but much of the result has to do with the application of the tool, which requires thinking.

A naïve approach would be to simply synchronize all of the methods that can be called from some client. This would mean, in the case of the `StatRecorderImpl`, that the `getRoster()` and `recordGame()` methods be declared as `synchronized`. But this would be a less than optimal approach because it is too broad (it would mean that you couldn't get the roster of two different teams at the same time).

What we really want to do is synchronize on the data structures that are going to get us into trouble. This means that we will place a lock on those data structures, and for the code that might cause trouble to run, it must get the lock. If all of the troublesome code is synchronized on the same data, then only one part of the code can run at a time. This is how we avoid these problems. But this is also tricky—if you lock for too long, you can kill your performance and increase the possibility of deadlock. Deadlock is the condition where two threads each hold a lock, and each needs a lock that the other is holding to proceed. Avoiding deadlock requires that you make sure that you don't lock too much (among other things).

In our example, we could decide to synchronize on the `Player` object while doing the update. But the updates happen at a lower level of granularity, so we should probably lock at that lower level. One way to approach our update would be to rewrite our `updateBatting()` method along the lines of:

```
/**
 * Update the batting statistics for a player for a particular game.
 * This method assumes that the player is associated with some batting
 * statistics (e.g., that there is a {@link Batter} object associated
 * with the player.)
 * @param batter Player whose batting statistics are to be updated
 * @param results a list of the batting results for a particular game
 */
private void updateBatting(Player batter, List<Batter.AtBatResult> results) {
    Batter batStats = batter.asBatter();
    synchronized (batter) {
        for (Batter.AtBatResult r : results) {
            batStats.atBat(r);
        }
    }
}
```

Changing the method in this way will ensure that no other thread can access the particular batter object while the `updateBatting()` method is running. Updates will be done one at a time, and rosters will need to wait until the update is done to gain access to the `Batter` (which is part of the `Player`). Doing the same sort of locking for the other updates should ensure that those calling `getRoster()` will at least see consistent statistics on particular players. It will still be possible to get a roster that has some players updated for a game that hasn't been recorded against other players, but that is something we can live with.

Adding locks to our code can ensure that only a single thread accesses the object that is locked, helping us to avoid some concurrency bugs. But as things get more complex, locking also introduces a new class of bugs that revolve around the locks themselves.

Suppose, for example, that we have implemented a way to update the fielding results for a game. Further, instead of just passing the batting results for a particular player into updateBatting(), we hand in a structure that contains both the batting and the fielding results. Likewise, for an updateFielding() method, we hand in the same structure. Because we are paranoid, at the end of updateBatting(), we call updateFielding() (assuming we have a way of checking whether it has already been called), and when we end the updateFielding() method, we call updateBatting() (also assuming that we can find out whether it has already been called).

This will work fine, up until the time that the statistics for the same player are simultaneously being updated by two threads, one of which is starting with the updateBatting() method and the other starting at the updateFielding() method. The thread starting with updateBatting() will get a lock on the BattingImpl object for the player at the same time the updateFielding() method gets the lock on the FieldingImpl object for the player. Then, each thread will wait to get the lock that the other is holding so that it can complete the update. Unfortunately, both threads will wait forever, since neither will yield the lock they currently have until they get the lock that the other is holding.

This is a classic case of deadlock, where progress in each thread is blocked because of a lock held by the other. Such deadlocks are not always consistent. They will not happen all the time, just when it is most inconvenient. Fortunately, deadlock is often easy to find because there will be two (or more) threads that are completely blocked. The good thing about deadlock is that when it happens, it stays in the deadlock state while you look at the thing.

Avoiding deadlock requires that when locking multiple objects for some operation, you know the right order in which to lock those objects. If all code accessing a particular group of objects tries to get locks in the same order, then deadlock can be avoided. But making sure that everyone in a large software project always acquires locks in the same order is a difficult coordination problem. It is the sort of thing that may be considered a style issue, but if you want a system that works, you had best all agree on that part of the style and enforce it in the code.

Holding locks for as little time as possible will minimize the likelihood of deadlock, so here is another reason to think hard about the scope of a lock. The longer you hold any lock, the more likely it is that you are holding someone else up. That will cut down on the efficiency of the program, but if the one who is waiting for you holds something that you need, then you will be in deadlock.

This is especially true if you are using RMI and doing some distributed processing. Such programs are inherently concurrent, in that both the program making an RMI call and the program receiving the RMI call will have a thread running. Although the two threads can't share the same data, they can make RMI calls themselves. So if I call a server and then the server calls back to me, we could each be waiting for the other, giving us a distributed deadlock. Unlike deadlock in a single process, which can be found using fairly standard tools, discovering distributed deadlock is very difficult. There are various ways you can try, but the general problem of finding such deadlocks is provably impossible. Your best bet is to never hold a lock when making a remote call, and making sure that no one else does so either.

As bad as deadlock is, it has an even more evil twin: livelock. Livelock occurs when two threads are contending for a resource, but react to that contention by doing something that also results in contention. Livelock cases tend to be more complex, but they are the coding equivalent of two people arriving at a doorway together. Each steps back to let the other through. On seeing the other step back, each tries to go through the door, and they collide. On collision, each steps back to let the other through. And the series repeats. Forever.

What makes livelock worse than deadlock is that even though no progress is being made, something is happening. This makes livelock harder to find: there are no threads that show up as stuck. It means that resources are being used. And just like deadlock, livelock is even harder to find in a distributed application. The only good thing about livelock is that it is much less common than deadlock. But it can happen, so you should be aware of the possibility.

This is only the briefest of introductions to the problems and techniques of writing thread-safe code. There are a number of interesting longer works on the subject,[||] and I highly recommend reading some of those before plunging into problems that require thread safety. The other thing to understand about programming with threads is that brute force (even brute force with a debugger) is not the way to be successful. You have to think, and think hard, about what could be going on in the program under all the different ways that it could execute. This is also an area where having your code reviewed by someone else can be a huge aid. There is nothing like a second set of eyes to help you find race conditions or potential deadlock.

Atomic Data

When we looked at the concurrency problems with the `StatRecorderImpl`, one set of assumptions that could have gotten us into trouble concerned the atomicity of the operations in some of the methods. Thinking that something as simple as incrementing an integer is thread-safe has been the cause of many concurrency bugs. Synchronizing such uses can keep our program correct, but the locking involved can be expensive.

To help in this, the Java libraries now contain a set of atomic data types. These objects can be used in place of the corresponding data types and provide thread safety in a

---

[||] My personal favorite is still Andrew Birrell's *An Introduction to Programming with Threads*, *https://birrell.org/andrew/papers/035-Threads.pdf*, recently updated so that the examples are in a more contemporary language, as well as *An Introduction to Programming with C# Threads*, *https://birrell.org/andrew/papers/ThreadsCSharp.pdf*. It is an indication of the complexity of this problem that the best paper on the subject was originally written in 1989. We have not progressed very far with respect to this problem in the last 30 years.

lock-free fashion. These objects also provide a number of methods that themselves are guaranteed to be atomic and because of that allow thread-safe manipulation of these data types.

Let's go back for a moment to our `StatRecorderImpl` and think about one of the reasons we needed to synchronize the `atBat()` method of the `BatterImpl` object. All that method does is increment a set of counters. But we couldn't be sure that those increments would be atomic, and not made incorrect when accessed by multiple threads. The `atomic` data objects in the `java.concurrent.atomic` package do ensure just such atomicity.

Using those data types for our `BatterImpl` would be possible, but a bit clumsy. We would need to change the declarations of the counters to look like:

```
private AtomicInteger atBats;
private AtomicInteger hits;
private AtomicInteger bases;
private AtomicInteger baseOnBalls;
private AtomicInteger sacrifices;
```

and the initialization of those fields in the constructor to:

```
public BatterImpl() {
        atBats = new AtomicInteger();
        hits = new AtomicInteger();
        bases = new AtomicInteger();
        baseOnBalls = new AtomicInteger();
        sacrifices = new AtomicInteger();
    }
```

The body of the `atBat()` method could then be changed to:

```
public void atBat(AtBatResult what) {
        switch (what) {
            case strikeOut:
                break;
            case fieldOut:
                break;
            case base1:
                hits.incrementAndGet();
                bases.incrementAndGet();
                break;
            case base2:
                hits.incrementAndGet();
                bases.addAndGet(2);
                break;
            case base3:
                hits.incrementAndGet();
                bases.addAndGet(3);
            case base4:
                hits.incrementAndGet();
                bases.addAndGet(4);
            case sacrifice:
                sacrifices.incrementAndGet();
                return;
            case walk:
```

```
                baseOnBalls.incrementAndGet();
                return;
        }
        atBats.incrementAndGet();
}
```

The reason to do this obviously is not for the code clarity. But these data objects are guaranteed to have atomic implementations of the various methods, so we can be sure that this implementation, even without the locking provided by synchronization, will result in correct statistics. This does not solve the problem of possibly returning an inconsistent statistic because a getRoster() call picks up a player that is in the middle of an atBat() update, but it keeps the data from being corrupted, which is a much more serious problem.

The atomic data items are very useful when you need to implement a multithreaded counter or need to make some comparison in a routine that might have multiple threads running through it. There is nothing that can be done with these that can't be done with synchronized over the right scope, but the atomic objects will probably perform better, and you don't have to think about the scope of the lock. Atomic objects should not be overused or (as we did earlier in this chapter) used for the wrong reasons. But when you need one of them, they can't be beat.

There are lots of other classes that can help with concurrency in Java programs. We haven't talked about the various kinds of lock classes that can be used, or the way in which the threads that you start can be controlled. Doing a thorough job of describing the richness of the concurrency constructs in the environment would take a separate book.#

What makes the concurrency mechanisms in the Java language and environment good is not, in general, that there is some new way of dealing with concurrency. It is still hard, and you still have to think about it, and debugging a concurrency problem in Java is just as much a hit-your-head-on-the-wall problem as it is in other languages. What makes Java concurrency different is that the language and the environment have some built-in help for all of the problems. You don't have to figure out how to build your own locking mechanism; there is the synchronized keyword. You don't have to find the right library to spawn new threads, since threads are part of the basic environment (and are first-class entities in the language itself). And, because threads are in the language, you don't have to figure out the different (and mind-bogglingly complex) libraries dealing with threads on the different platforms that you need to support; you can simply let the JVM implementation cover over those facts for you.

Of which there are many. My favorite is Doug Lea's *Concurrent Programming in Java* (Addison Wesley), but there are others that are also good.

Concurrent programming is the next frontier for languages and software engineering. Because of the advent of multicore systems, those of us who used to be able to ignore concurrent programming will no longer have that option. We are going to have to understand concurrency, and over time, we will no doubt invent idioms and practices that will make the programming of concurrent systems easier and more stylized. Until that happens, though, it is good to have a language and environment that you can trust to do the right thing if you have written the right program. Java may not have the ultimate answer to writing with multiple threads, but it has an answer that you can use to your advantage to deal with the new chips. That by itself makes this one of the good parts.

CHAPTER 11

The Developer Ecology

There was a time, not all that long ago, when developers faced the vast emptiness of an unwritten program carrying only the simple tools of an editor, a compiler, and (if they were lucky) a debugger. Like their spiritual forefathers who carved a country out of the forests with just an axe and a flintlock, these hardy developers built things of lasting beauty with remarkably crude tools. Get a bunch of older developers together and they will soon be talking about the deprivations of those times, and how programmers these days have it soft and don't really know what it was like to wait for hours to get a compile done or to track down a subtle bug with nothing but their bare hands and `printf`.

But we are no longer in the frontier times of software development. Indeed, there is a thriving ecology around tools for the software developer, especially around the Java language and environment. Although there are still remarkable craftsmen (and craftswomen) building software using the coding equivalents of axes and flintlocks, developers now have a selection of power tools that make things easier and aid in the production of good software. These aren't really part of the Java language or runtime, but many of these tools have grown up around the language and runtime. So our final look at the good parts of Java will be to take a quick tour of some of these tools and talk a bit about how they can improve a developer's life.

Technically, we have already talked about one of these tools. Javadoc, singled out as one of the good parts of the Java environment, is really a separate tool for generating documentation. But it is so important, and so tightly integrated with the language itself, that it deserved its own chapter. Some of the tools that we will look at in this chapter can save the developer just as much time and effort, and so are important to know and use. New tools are being added to the environment all the time, so what follows is a partial and idiosyncratic list. But the very fact that tools are constantly being developed and added to the ecology around the Java environment is an indication of the vitality of the technology. As the language and runtime have evolved, the innovation has moved away from new language features or new approaches to the virtual machine and toward the tools that make using the language and VM easier and more productive.

IDEs

Nothing is as indicative of a generation gap amongst programmers than the use of IDEs (which, depending on who you talk to, is an acronym for either interactive development environment or interactive debugging environment).* As a rule, older programmers tend to stay with a separate editor, compile in a shell, and debug with a third tool. Younger programmers tend to have a single environment in which they do all three of these, and much more. I was certainly a member of the older generation for a long time, and for good reason—the commands of an editor become hardcoded into one's fingertips, and learning a different environment, even if it eventually offers more functionality, will cut down on your immediate productivity.

But I now have trouble even imagining what it would be like to develop a system without the aids offered by an IDE. In some sense, these environments are a simple combination of editor, compiler, and debugger. But in fact they go well beyond those simple functions, supplying lots of additional information along the way that used to require using multiple tools simultaneously and lots of context switching.

When I first started using an IDE,† I was using Eclipse, which still seems to be the most popular of the open source tools. For the past couple of years, I've been using Netbeans. Although comparing IDEs has become the equivalent of comparing editors in terms of the religious fervor of those who use them, I find at least these two are pretty much comparable (although not, interestingly, always compatible). Each of these does some things slightly better than the other, each has a model of work that is largely the same (until it isn't), and each has a rather healthy group of contributors moving the tool forward. In what follows, I usually will be talking about my experience with Netbeans.

IDEs now offer both code completion and online documentation as part of the editing process. While entering your code, the IDE will (upon a configurable pause) show you which possible set of methods or fields could be the completion of your partial typing, and allow you to pick one of those completions rather than continuing typing. Pausing over a method call should bring up the javadoc for that method. Typing in a method call will give you a template for the arguments needed for the method. All the while, the IDE is parsing the code on the fly, allowing you to see whether the code will compile properly while you edit. The IDE will even keep track of your `import` statements, automatically importing the classes you need and flagging imports that are not used.

---

* That we now have acronyms for which no one really knows the full form is an indication that the whole acronym thing has gotten even more completely out of hand than we had suspected.

† There are many commercially available IDEs on the market, but it appears that the two most commonly used IDEs for Java development are the open source projects Eclipse (*http://www.eclipse.org*) and Netbeans (*http://www.netbeans.org*). I'm not trying to say which one is better, as life is too short for those sorts of discussions and I've already spent way too much time in said discussions as it is. Pick the one you like. Your mileage may vary. Satisfaction guaranteed or I won't be surprised. Please send all further correspondence on this subject to */dev/null*.

The IDE will also format your code, which is an easy way to ensure that all members of a team use reasonably consistent formatting style.

IDEs also have facilities to aid in common refactoring processes. If you need to rename some class, field, or method, the IDE can make the changes through an entire set of source files. If you decide to break a class into two different classes or split an interface, these IDEs can make the change throughout your code. Lots of tasks that used to take a script utilizing `find` and `sed` (and a day or two of debugging said script) can now be done in the IDE. The advantage is that the IDE actually knows something about the language being altered, and so can do a far more intelligent job than the scripts could do.

IDEs are a great help when writing your own code, but they are invaluable when you are reading code written by someone else. This is because the IDE provides navigation functions that can't be provided by a simple editor. IDEs scan and parse an entire set of related Java files, and can be set up so that all of the dependencies of a particular program can be included in the scan. From this, the IDE can form a dependency tree of the entire program or system. This allows navigation directly to the source that declares or defines some other class. When hunting through code that you didn't write (or that you wrote some time ago), these navigation aids are invaluable.

The IDEs will also let you maintain the build files for your system (and let you use any of the usual suspects for building, such as Make, Ant, or Maven), and let you run and debug your system from the editor itself. All of which is highly convenient, saves time, and can help you avoid the problem of finding a bug within the debugger and then forgetting exactly where that bug was when you switch over to your editor.

In fact, these IDEs have introduced into the Java environment the kind of programming systems that users of LISP used years ago and were the basis for those folks claiming the inherent superiority of LISP.[‡] Rather than development having the old rhythm of edit/compile/debug, with each phase being separate and each requiring a different set of tools (and each phase being separated by considerable chunks of time), the IDEs now available merge the edit/compile/debug cycle into a continuous workflow. Programming becomes far more interactive, since simple mistakes can be caught on the fly. Even better, design decisions are far easier to revisit, since you can refactor your code with the aid of the tools and hence don't pay the kinds of penalties that we used to pay for making a bad decision early on in the development process.

All of these advantages accrue even if your development is (like mine) low-level system code. If you are doing development using one of the many Java frameworks or containers or are building graphical interfaces, the IDEs are even more of a laborsaving device, as they have integrated tools that will generate most of the boilerplate code

---

[‡] LISP programmers are always happy to tell you just how much better LISP was than anything before or since, how much better it was as a development language, and how all the advances that have occurred since then are just attempts at recreating what they had 30 years ago. Even if they are right, they need to let it go.

needed for these tasks. Not using these tools when doing such tasks is like trying to start a fire by banging rocks together.

This is not to say that everything is perfect with these tools. I have had, well…interesting experiences with the way IDEs interface with revision control systems. The view of what code is appropriate may strike some as a bit fascistic. And the user interface—well, let's just say this is the sort of interface that could only have been produced by programmers on an open source project. Everything can be configured and changed, which is the good news. And most everything *needs* to be configured and changed, which is the bad news.

Still, these are great tools, and their rapid evolution and improvement over time is a testament to the open source development model they have adopted. If you still want to write your code with an editor, then there is little I can do to convince you that life could be better otherwise. But if you spend time working with code that has been written by someone else, you owe it to yourself to become familiar with at least one of these IDEs. Even if you spend all of your time with code that you write, it is probably worth your time to try one of the IDEs on a project. You might be surprised to find that they are useful.

JUnit

Writing tests for your code is the software equivalent of flossing. Everyone knows that they should do it, everyone knows what bad things will happen if they don't do it, and yet very few people do it. After all, management is always after you to produce new functionality, and writing tests slows you down from doing that. And a lot of the code you have written is so simple that nothing could go wrong, so writing tests just wastes precious time. And writing tests is boring, and not much fun, and sometimes is really hard. And the best thing that can happen when you write a test is that you find out your code was right to begin with. Most of the time it just shows that there are problems, which you have to go back and fix before you can work on the exciting new stuff.

It is when a junior engineer gets to this point that I roll up a newspaper and start swatting him with it.§ We all know that unless code is tested, it has bugs.‖ Testing may be hard, but it need not be boring, and it is absolutely necessary. Remember that what Java is good for is the building of large-scale, long-lived, reliable systems. Such systems need lots and lots of tests, both to ensure that they are right in the first place and to keep them right as they evolve over time.

§ The point isn't to hurt the engineer being swatted, but just to make a loud enough noise that it scares him. Unless I've done this to him before, in which case I use something much harder than a rolled-up newspaper.

‖ From which it does not follow that if the code is tested, it does not have bugs. But it will probably have fewer bugs, and that's the point.

Fortunately, there are good tools to help you build tests for your Java code. These testing frameworks give you a way to build and run your tests, and will even generate some of the boilerplate code for you. My current favorite is JUnit.# It is free, open source, and simple, all of which are features that I find appealing. Even better, it is integrated into most of the IDEs, so there is already support in the environment for writing tests. It may not make writing tests as much fun as writing the code that is being tested, but it helps enough that even those who are test averse might be inclined to do the right thing.

JUnit works by marking your test code with the annotation @Test. It also allows you to define a method that will be called before the tests are run, so that you can set up a test environment, and after the tests are completed, allows you to clean up. In between, the tests that you define in a class will be run.

Evaluation of the tests can be done in a couple of ways. The simplest is to end the test by checking that the expected outcome was achieved, by using the JUnit class Assert. This class gives you a large number of methods that can compare the result of your test run with the value that you expect. If the assertion is true, the test is recorded as passing; if it is false, the test is recorded as failing. The other mechanism that can be exploited is, again, an annotation. Methods can be marked with the @Test expected annotation, which tests to see whether the appropriate runtime exception is thrown by the method.

We have seen JUnit before, when I first talked about testing. If you recall, we wrote a test to make sure that the implementation of the method that got the slugging percentage for a Batter object would give an answer that was consistent with the number of at-bats and the number of bases totaled for that Batter. To refresh your memory, the code looked like:

```
/**
 * Test method for
 * {@link org.oreilly.javaGoodParts.examples.impl.BatterImpl#getSlugging()}.
 * This method will take the array of Batter objects stored in the private
 * variable testBatters and made sure that all of them are consistent with
 * regards to the slugging percentage, the number of at-bats, and the total
 * number of bases recorded.
 */
@Test
public void testGetSlugging() {
    for (int i = 0; i < testBatters.length; i++) {
        try {
            float testAvg = testBatters[i].getSlugging();
            float calcAvg = (float)testBatters[i].getTotalBases()
                    / (float) testBatters[i].getAtBats();
                assertEquals("Slugging test", testAvg, calcAvg, .02);
```

#See *http://junit.sourceforge.net/*. JUnit is the brainchild of Kent Beck and Erich Gamma. Enough said.

```
            } catch (NotEnoughAtBatsException e) {
                assertEquals("Slugging exception", true,
                        (10 == (e.getNeeded() + testBatters[i].getAtBats()))));
            }
        }
    }
```

We have marked this method with the @Test annotation. We assume that an array of objects that support the Batter interface has been initialized elsewhere, and go through that array and check that the slugging percentage is consistent with the at-bats and the total number of bases. We use a particular version of the assertEquals() method that allows us to supply a range of accuracy that we consider acceptable. In this case, we consider a variation of .02 between the reported averages to be acceptable.

Setting up the array of objects used in this test can be done in a method marked with the annotation @Before, which will be run by the JUnit framework before the other tests. This method can call out to other methods if needed, and is often the most difficult part of writing the test, since this is where you will create the data on which the tests will depend. For our case, we might start our test file with something like:

```
package org.oreilly.javaGoodParts.examples.impl;

import static org.junit.Assert.*;

import java.util.HashMap;
import java.util.Random;

import org.junit.After;
import org.junit.Before;
import org.junit.Test;
import org.oreilly.javaGoodParts.examples.statistics.NotEnoughAtBatsException;
import org.oreilly.javaGoodParts.examples.statistics.Batter.AtBatResult;

/**
 *
 */
public class BatterImplTest {
    private BatterImpl[] testBatters;
    private Random dataGen = new Random(1);

    /**
     * Set up the test array testBatters. We will test on 100 {@link BatterImpl}
     * objects. These will each be initialized in a separate routine.
     */
    @Before
    public void setUp() {
        testBatters = new BatterImpl[100];
        for (int i = 0; i < 100; i++) {
            testBatters[i] = new BatterImpl();
            initBatter(testBatters[i]);
        }
        System.out.println("Test setup successfully complete");
    }
```

```
/**
 * Initialize the test cases that will be used for these tests. Each object
 * will be given a random number of at-bats ranging from 0-100; if the
 * number of at-bats is less than 10, we increment the number by 10 to
 * ensure that each test case has the minimum number of at-bats. Then each
 * at-bat will be given a random result, which will be recorded by a call to
 * the {@link BatterImpl.atBat()} method.
 *
 * @param batterImpl
 *                  The batter object being initialized
 */
private void initBatter(BatterImpl batter) {
    int numbats;
    HashMap<Integer, AtBatResult> resultsTable
        = new HashMap<Integer, AtBatResult>();

    resultsTable.put(0, AtBatResult.strikeOut);
    resultsTable.put(1, AtBatResult.fieldOut);
    resultsTable.put(2, AtBatResult.base1);
    resultsTable.put(3, AtBatResult.base2);
    resultsTable.put(4, AtBatResult.base3);
    resultsTable.put(5, AtBatResult.base4);
    resultsTable.put(6, AtBatResult.walk);
    resultsTable.put(7, AtBatResult.reachOnError);
    resultsTable.put(8, AtBatResult.sacrifice);

    numbats = dataGen.nextInt(100);
    if (numbats < 10)
        numbats++;
    for (int i = 0; i < numbats; i++) {
        batter.atBat(resultsTable.get(dataGen.nextInt(9)));
    }
}
```

This will give us an array of 100 batter objects that we can use to test all of our methods that return batting statistics. We randomly assign a number of at-bats for each batter, but make sure that each has at least the minimum number needed to get a real average. We then generate a random result for each of these at bats. We build a simple HashTable to allow us to translate between our random integer value and an at-bat result. Note that we plan on using the atBat() method in the Batter interface to initialize these records, so we will need to test that method using some other data set. That set will need to feed a known set of at-bat combinations to batter objects, and then see whether the resulting statistics reflect the known state of the input, If that test works, we will be able to trust (more) the tests we are running that depend on the correctness of the atBat() method.

Our initialization is pretty simple, only creating local objects that we can leave to the garbage collector to clean up. If we were doing something that used resources such as file descriptors or sockets, however, we would need to clean up after ourselves at the end of the test run. To do this, JUnit looks for a method with the annotation @After. Don't neglect to write this method if you are using limited resources in your tests, as there is no guarantee that your tests will be run by themselves. JUnit is set up to run groups of tests together, so yours might be part of a much larger test run. You might not use up all of the resources on the test machine, but if you keep any after your test run and others do the same, the cumulative effect may be to build a test suite that is itself unreliable.

Sometimes it takes a lot of code to do a reasonable test. This is especially true for code like the `StatRecorder` and `StatReporter` that we saw earlier that forms a client-server system meant to operate over the network. To test either of these requires that we emulate the other side of the network inside of our tests. This doesn't mean that we have to reimplement either the client or the server, but we do need a local implementation of code that will take the appropriate inputs and give the appropriate outputs. Since the test code knows the kinds of inputs and outputs expected, this can be considerably easier than reimplementing the whole of the client and server. But it does take some thought.

Writing good test suites is a subject that is often ignored, but is an interesting programming problem in its own right. This subject has gotten more interest with the advocacy of test-driven development, but it really doesn't matter whether you write the tests before the code, or the code and then the tests, as long as both get written. Coming up with a really good test suite is a difficult design problem that is often as challenging as writing the code being tested. I won't go further into the subject here.* But good tests can make your system more reliable, easier to change, and easier to understand. The great thing about JUnit is that it makes those tests easier to write, assemble into suites, and run.

FindBugs

We've written our code. We've written a lot of tests for that code. If we are developing as part of a team,† we've had at least one other member of the team review the code *and* the tests, which has led to some changes in both the code and the tests. Having gone through all that, we can be sure that our code is bug-free, right?

Unfortunately, no. No matter how careful we are, there is always some bug that has made it through our scrutiny, slipped by the tests, and gone unnoticed by our reviewers. So we should be on the lookout for any tool that attempts to help us find the bugs that might otherwise get away.

---

* For those who do want to gain some appreciation for what it is to write a good test suite, I can think of no better stimulus to your thinking than Alberto Savoia's marvelous "Beautiful Tests," a chapter in Oram and Wilson's *Beautiful Code* (http://oreilly.com/catalog/9780596510046/.)

† Really thorough code reviews, in which someone else reads your code carefully to find problems, are the best way I know to do early bug detection. But they are rarely done. This is partly because they take a lot of time to do well, but I think it is mainly because most programmers are a bit afraid of having someone else review their source. We as a profession need to get over this reluctance; if you don't want someone to read your code, then write it so you do. If someone else shouldn't read it, why should someone else use it?

One of the more interesting of such tools is FindBugs,‡ developed at the University of Maryland by a group originally led by Bill Pugh and David Hovemeyer. The idea behind the project is that certain patterns in code are *likely* to indicate a bug in the code. FindBugs is a program that does static analysis looking for such patterns and reports the results back to the user. FindBugs is not a style checker; the code that it looks at is the binary output of your source. It operates on Java bytecodes, finding the likely bug patterns in that representation.

I tend to think of FindBugs as the Java-age equivalent of the old C `lint` program. Back in the day, you would run your C code through `lint` to find all of the problems that the compiler would happily ignore, such as casting a structure from one type to another. Sometimes `lint` would report problems that weren't really there; after all, there were times when you did want to cast from one type to another. But it was worth taking a look if `lint` reported something problematic to make sure that you really wanted to do what it was reporting as fishy.

In the same way, FindBugs will do a static analysis of your Java code and report places where there might be a bug. When FindBugs reports a problem, what it is doing is reporting a possible problem; it doesn't know that the code in question is wrong, but it relies on the knowledge that patterns like this code are often the cause of a problem. Just as `lint` would sometimes warn you against doing something that in fact you meant to do, running FindBugs will result in some false-positive reports. The developers of FindBugs try to minimize the number of false-positives, but they are working in a realm that is not well understood, and so have to rely on heuristics and statistical experience for their indicators. The Java language and compiler already do a reasonable job of eliminating problems that are certain to produce bugs, such as memory problems or illegal type casts. FindBugs moves to a new frontier, attempting to detect likely bugs.

I like to run FindBugs fairly late in the development cycle, after the tests have been successfully run and another engineer has reviewed the code. It is a final check on the code, allowing me to find and look at those parts of my program that might be problematic. At that point, I'm willing to deal with some false-positives, since finding even one or two genuine bugs is a big win. It might be that the real value of FindBugs is in the stimulus it gives for a final look at the code, although there are times when looking at the places it reports has given me a real "Aha!" moment.

The other thing that I like about FindBugs is that it started its life as an academic project, so there are papers explaining the approach and the ideas underlying this kind of bug detection. Knowing why some decisions are made is an important part of building trust in a tool like this. Of course, the project is also open source, so one can always look at the source to find out what is really going on. But I find the papers a more manageable way of understanding the basic ideas, and so appreciate having both.

‡ You can get FindBugs at *http://findbugs.sourceforge.net*.

Other Tools

The tools discussed in this chapter are exemplars of a more general trend. Surrounding the Java language, there is an increasingly diverse and rich set of tools for the development of software. Open source communities, either sponsored by a company (or set of companies) or coming out of academia, do much of the development for this ecology of software tools. The quality can be variable, but is generally quite good. Support happens via email or in public forums, which makes some companies nervous, but which in my experience is far superior to the kinds of paid-for support that you get with more standard commercial offerings.

There is a particular theme to the tools we have looked at in this chapter, having to do with the software cycle of writing code, testing that code, and eliminating bugs in the code. There are additional tools that go further into this cycle. For example, Checkstyle§ is a tool that will automate the checking of stylistic features in your code, and is a great way of enforcing a particular style guide. How many automated checks you want to include in your development process is up to you and the rest of your team, as is the set of checks that you want to have flagged by these tools (all of them are configurable and customizable).

I have not even touched on the other classes of tools that can be used for software development. Configuration management tools such as Ant‖ or Maven# offer Java-aware alternatives to make. Source code control systems such as Subversion* and Mercurial† allow teams to share their source trees in a distributed fashion. Continuous build tools such as Hudson‡ automate the process of building, testing, and reporting when changes are committed. The list of such tools goes on and on; trying to give even a brief review of them would take up another book of this size, and would be out of date by the time the book was in print.

The point to all this is that there is a thriving software ecology around tools that make Java development easier and aid in the production of fully tested, bug-minimized code.§ The combination of the ubiquity of the Java platform, the open source movement, and the distribution mechanism of the Web means that developers can write the tools that they need without having to justify their investment via a business plan or

---

§ See *http://checkstyle.sourceforge.net*.

‖ See *http://ant.apache.org*.

See *http://maven.apache.org*.

* See *http://subversion.tigris.org*.

† See *http://mercurial.selenic.com/*.

‡ See *http://hudson-ci.org*.

§ Note that I'm not claiming that the code will be bug-free; the only time code is in that state is when it hasn't been written. Bug-free is an ideal state that we can strive to achieve; bug minimization is an actual goal that we can reach.

market projection. Developers know what they need, and if one developer needs something, it is likely that others will find that thing useful as well. The user interfaces may not be polished and the documentation may be minimal, but these tools aid in our work and are worth the time investment to find and learn.

Of course, there is also a lot of crap out there. Just because a developer has written some code and is willing to give it away doesn't mean that the code is going to meet your needs, be stable, or work. There are many examples of offerings to the community and the ecology that are attempts to codify a particular developer's prejudice on how code should be written, developed, or used. Many of the prejudices are odd, if not simply wrong. Like any software, tools found in the Java ecology will vary in quality and usefulness, so you will need to check each one to find out whether it works for you. There is a lot of chaff out there, but the occasional bits of wheat can help make your life better.

The other point is that whatever tool it is that you need as you develop your code, you can probably find it on the Web already. It may not be exactly what you want, but if it is open source, you can make the changes so that it is. Just as the collections library in Java means that developers should not need to write their own basic data structures, the ecology of Java tools means that we generally don't need to write our own development support. And that is always a good thing.

The ecology is more than just tools. You can find prewritten libraries of Java code that do lots of things, from graphics to databases to agent systems. Again, some of these are good and others less so. There is still work involved in using these libraries, but this is rarely as much work as writing the code yourself if you weren't using the library. The trade-offs between using (and perhaps bending) existing code and writing from scratch will differ from programmer to programmer and from library to library. The simpler the code, the easier it is to understand and trust, but the less time it would take to write it yourself. Really complex code may be trusted only because of its reputation. Most programmers underestimate the amount of time it would take them to write some bit of functionality, and many would rather write code than read a manual or documentation for some existing code. Nonetheless, you can save time, effort, and money by taking a look around to see what is available prior to diving into the coding yourself.

The power of this ecology is hard to overestimate. All of the tools and code that already exist and that are freely available act as a force multiplier for each member of the Java community. In some sense, this has nothing to do with the language and the environment itself. This kind of ecology could have developed around any language (and, in fact, most languages now have some sort of ecology like this). What makes the Java ecology so good is the sheer size of the thing. Although making the right choices about what parts of that ecology to use may be difficult, having all of those choices makes a huge difference in your productivity. Spend some of the time that you save by using the ecology to explore the ecology, and perhaps to contribute to it. This is one of those cases where more really is more, and everyone wins.

Index

Symbols

We'd like to hear your suggestions for improving our indexes. Send email to *index@oreilly.com*.

175

cowboy example, 18
CPUs, multicore, 145

D

data, atomic data, 158–161
deadlocks, 157
declaring
    arguments, 16
    collections, 99
    exceptions, 23
    methods, 10
    packages, 39
    return values, 16
deserializing objects, 137
documentation (see Javadoc)
documentation comments
    about, 78
    tags, 79

E

efficiency, interfaces, 9
examples
    baseball statistics
        collections, 91–118
        concurrency, 148–160
        exceptions, 24–27, 29–33, 37
        garbage collection, 53–55, 56–61
        Javadoc, 80–88
        JUnit, 167–170
        JVM, 69–75
        packages, 44–46
        RMI, 122–138
        type system, 11–16, 18
    cowboy, 18
exceptions, 23–38
    about, 24–27
    baseball statistics example, 24–27, 29–33
    defining, 46
    programming practices, 33–36
    RemoteException, 133
    Runtime exceptions, 37–38, 98
    uses of, 27–29
extending classes, 7

F

fields
    private, public, and protected, 42
    static fields, 20

File class, 72
filesystems
    IDEs, 48
    JVM, 71
    packages, 46–48
finalizers, garbage collection, 56–61
FindBugs, 170

G

Gabriel, Richard, on "worse is better", 1
garbage collection, 49–62
    about, 50
    other resources, 56–62
    references, 51–55
generics
    about, 99
    parameterized types, 102

H

HashSet, 95
hierarchies, packages, 43
HTML, Javadoc, 79

I

IDEs (integrated development environments)
    about, 164
    documentation comments, 79
    filesystem, 48
implementation documentation, 85
import statement, 41
inheritance, 7
{@inheritDoc} tag, 85
interfaces
    about, 8
    access specifications, 43
    documenting, 82
    List interface, 93
    namespaces, 19
    RMI, 122
    semantics of, 12
    Set interface, 95, 100
    uses of, 10, 16
    using, 9
Iterator objects, 97

J

Java Generics, 99

Java, uses for, 3–5
java.util package, 91, 92
Javadoc, 77–89
    about, 78–80
    baseball statistics example, 80–88
JUnit
    about, 166–170
    baseball statistics example, 13
JVM (Java virtual machine), 63–76
    about, 63–66
    portability, 67–76
    security, 66

L

libraries
    collections library, 91
    Java code, 173
{@link} tag, 85
List interface, 93
livelocks, 158
loading classes, 20
locks, 156

M

marshalling objects, 139
memory
    garbage collection, 50
    leaks, 53–55
methods
    about, 7
    declaring, 10
    exceptions, 23
    private, public, and protected, 42
    semantics, 13
multicore chips, 145
multithreading, 146

N

name-equivalence languages, 137
namespaces
    interfaces, 19
    packages, 40
naming conventions, packages, 40
Network Objects, 140

O

object serialization

example, 135
    RMI, 134–143
objects, 7
    (see also classes)
    garbage collection, 50
    Iterator objects, 97
    Registry objects, 130
    UUID objects, 125
overrides, 7

P

package documentation, 86
package-info.java file, 88
packages, 39–48
    about, 39–42
    access control, 42
    baseball statistics example, 44–46
    filesystems, 46–48
parameterized types, 98–104
Pascal, compared to JVM, 65
performance, interfaces, 9
polymorphic type systems
    about, 7
    exceptions, 26
portability
    bytecodes, 3
    JVM, 67–76
private fields or methods, 42
processors, multicore, 145
programming practices
    classes and type system, 16
    exceptions, 28, 33–36, 33
    garbage collection, 50
    Javadoc, 79
    managing resources, 56
    memory leaks, 53
    packages, 40
protected fields or methods, 43
public fields or methods, 43

R

random access, collections, 114–118
refactoring
    about, 45
    using IDEs, 165
references
    garbage collection, 51–55
    security, 52

Registry objects, 130
relationships, type system, 15
RemoteException, 133
resources, managing with garbage collection, 56–62
return values, declaring, 16
RMI (Remote Method Invocation), 121–143
    about, 122–134
    concurrency, 146
    object serialization, 134–139
    subtypes, 139–143
Runtime exceptions, 37–38, 98

S

security
    JVM, 66
    references, 52
    static fields, 20
semantics
    interfaces, 12
    methods, 13
serialVersionUID, 137
servers, client and server agreements, 133
Set interface, 95, 100
static fields, security flaw, 20
statistics package, 105–110
subtypes, RMI, 139–143
synchronization, concurrency, 152–158

T

tags
    documentation comments, 79
    {@inheritDoc} tag, 85
    {@link} tag, 85
testing, JUnit, 166
threads
    defined, 147
    synchronization, 152
Throwable class, 24
type parameters, declaring collections, 99
type system, 7–21
    (see also classes; inheritance; methods; objects)
    about, 7–9
    applets, 20
    baseball statistics example, 11–16, 18
    cowboy example, 18
    declarations, 16

namespaces and interfaces, 19
parameterized types, 98–104
programming practices using classes, 16

U

UCSD Pascal, compared to JVM, 65
unmarshalling objects, 139
UUID objects, 125

V

values, return values, 16
verification, JVM, 66
virtual machines, 63
    (see also JVM)

W

Waldo, Jim, personal history with Java, viii
Wollrath, Ann, RPC systems, 122
"worse is better", 1

About the Author

Jim Waldo is a Distinguished Engineer with Sun Microsystems Laboratories, where he investigates next-generation large-scale distributed systems. He is currently the technical lead of Project Darkstar, a multithreaded, distributed infrastructure for massive multiplayer online games and virtual worlds. Prior to his current assignment with Sun Labs, he was the lead architect for Jini, a distributed programming system based on Java.

Before joining Sun, Jim spent eight years at Apollo Computer and Hewlett Packard working in the areas of distributed object systems, user interfaces, class libraries, text, and internationalization. While at HP, he led the design and development of the first Object Request Broker, and he was instrumental in getting that technology incorporated into the first OMG CORBA specification.

Jim is a Professor of the Practice at Harvard University, where he teaches distributed computing and topics in the intersection of policy and technology in the department of computer science.

Jim received his Ph.D. in philosophy from the University of Massachusetts (Amherst). He also holds M.A. degrees in both linguistics and philosophy from the University of Utah. He is a member of the IEEE and ACM.

Colophon

The animal on the cover of *Java: The Good Parts* is a black giant squirrel (*Ratufa bicolor*), formerly known as a Javan squirrel (*Sciurus javensis*). It is also referred to today as a Malayan giant squirrel or jelerang. This species can be found throughout southeast Asia, though its range has diminished due to deforestation. It lives in the high forest canopy, foraging during the day for wild fruit and nuts.

One of the largest squirrels in the world, the black giant squirrel's tail is slightly longer than its body. Taking this into account, its average length is two to three feet. There is a clear color separation between the squirrel's back (deep brown or black) and the cream abdomen, giving rise to the "bicolor" in its Latin name. The squirrels' long tails are used as a counterweight to help them balance on branches. It is also notable that in their basic posture, the tail hangs limp rather than curling upright (as is the case with other tree squirrels).

Though it lives in the depths of the forest and tends to be reclusive, the black giant squirrel is easily tamed and frequently kept as a pet. It is also a food source for natives; in fact, as of 2008, it is listed as a near-threatened species due to overhunting, as well as habitat loss.

The cover image is from Wood's *Animate Creations*. The cover font is Adobe ITC Garamond. The text font is Linotype Birka; the heading font is Adobe Myriad Condensed; and the code font is LucasFont's TheSansMonoCondensed.

Buy this book and get access to the online edition for 45 days—for free!

Java: The Good Parts
By Jim Waldo
April 2010, $29.99
ISBN 9780596803735

With Safari Books Online, you can:

Access the contents of thousands of technology and business books

- Quickly search over 7000 books and certification guides
- Download whole books or chapters in PDF format, at no extra cost, to print or read on the go
- Copy and paste code
- Save up to 35% on O'Reilly print books
- **New!** Access mobile-friendly books directly from cell phones and mobile devices

Stay up-to-date on emerging topics before the books are published

- Get on-demand access to evolving manuscripts.
- Interact directly with authors of upcoming books

Explore thousands of hours of video on technology and design topics

- Learn from expert video tutorials
- Watch and replay recorded conference sessions

To try out Safari and the online edition of this book FREE for 45 days, go to **www.oreilly.com/go/safarienabled** and enter the coupon code LFSSREH. To see the complete Safari Library, visit safari.oreilly.com.

Spreading the knowledge of innovators   safari.oreilly.com